# How to MAKE a DIFFERENCE

# How to MAKE a DIFFERENCE

### OVER 1,000 WAYS TO SERVE AT HOME, IN YOUR COMMUNITY, AND IN THE WORLD

## CATHERINE E. POELMAN

SHADOW
MOUNTAIN

Visit us at www.shadowmountain.com

Library of Congress Cataloging-in-Publication Data

Poelman, Catherine E., 1943–
   How to make a difference : over 1,000 ways to serve at home, in the community, and in the world / Catherine E. Poelman.
     p.    cm.
   Includes bibliographical references and index.
   ISBN 1-57008-874-8 (pbk.)
   1. Volunteerism.   2. Helping behavior.   3. Social service.   I. Title.
HN49.V64 P64 2002
302'.14—dc21                                      2002010862

Printed in the United States of America         72076-6992
Publishers Printing, Salt Lake City, UT

10  9   8   7   6   5   4   3   2   1

*For Jim, Pat, and Kathleen,*
*whose service at Shriners Hospital*
*is the embodiment of shared vision.*

# CONTENTS

# PREFACE

Four months after the vicious September 11th attack on America, President George W. Bush stood before the nation and issued a challenge—one intended to heal, help, and hold our country together through future times of trouble. He asked every American to "commit at least two years—4,000 hours over the rest of your lifetime—to the service of your neighbors and your nation.

"Our country . . . needs citizens working to rebuild our communities," the president said. "We need mentors to love children, especially children whose parents are in prison. And we need more talented teachers in troubled schools" (29 January 2002).

Essentially, what this country needs are people who are willing to make a difference. People like eight-year-old Austin Rogers of Lakewood, Washington. Austin had been given six dollars at school after learning about the parable of the talents from the New Testament. With the six bills in his pocket and a challenge to make the most of his money, Austin visited a number of shops and stores. His goal: purchase a few small items to give away to children at a homeless shelter. At each location, however, Austin's money was not accepted. Instead, a supermarket donated a cart of baby food and other essentials. The local bookstore owner gave Austin fifty-seven dollars worth of new books. Austin still gave his six dollars to the homeless shelter, but they were accompanied by books, baby food, and other donated items. Austin's mother said that he didn't think what he did was really so special; it's just what people are supposed to do for others. Yet he certainly made a difference to the mom who had something to feed her baby and to the child who was comforted with a story.

This book is all about making a difference—to your family, your community, the nation, and the world. How you choose to serve may differ from Austin's choice. You may want to do something simple or something grand or even several things in between. Whatever the form, your service will be an answer to the president's challenge and a step forward for our nation. As President Bush declared, "This time of adversity offers a unique moment of opportunity—a moment we must seize to change our culture. Through the gathering momentum of millions of acts of service and decency and kindness, I know we can overcome evil with greater good."

# GETTING STARTED

*You must give some time to your fellow man. Even if it's a little thing, do something for those who have need of help, something for which you get no pay but the privilege of doing it.*

—*Albert Schweitzer*

As individuals, we are incomplete without touching others' lives. A person who doesn't care about others faces an existence without joy. But a person who is genuinely helpful, charitable, and compassionate can awaken hope in another. Indeed, those who serve develop infinite appreciation and respect for a wide assortment of individuals.

Our modern world, however, is geared to efficiency. Commitment to serve rarely fits comfortably into pressing time schedules and increasing budget constraints. But if we open our lives to the service of others, we find that serving provides moral grounding, enlivens creativity, and spreads the responsibility for civic progress. Reading this book is the first indicator that you know the power of service and want to make a difference—even if it is small—in your own life, in your community, and in the world. As you discover the vast number of areas in which your own skills and personality can work for good, you will be filled with ideas for serving others; and those ideas will push you toward action, changing your life and the lives of everyone around you.

## STARTING SMALL

Service is more about kindness than perfection, smiles than solemnity, and restraint than excess. The most effective service begins small and close to home. Anyone can do the small things.

And doing them will bring sustainable happiness and personal fulfillment. To start small, simply remember that everyone in this world has the same basic need: to love and to be loved. Each individual is a child of God; human kinship is our connection to each other; and serving another person is an act of love.

You don't have to work at a homeless shelter, or be a member of the Red Cross, or become a volunteer firefighter to make a difference to those around you. Serving within your own sphere of influence is just as vital. So, when you start to feel that you are not doing as much as you should, do a reality check and remember:

• Helping children in an elementary school learn to read is no more important than reading with your own child.

• Entertaining the elderly at a nursing home is no more important than visiting your elderly neighbor.

• Feeding the homeless is no more important than feeding the family whose mother is in chemotherapy.

• Giving malaria shots to Kenyans is no more important than giving flu shots to low-income seniors.

• Clearing trails in Alaska is no more important than adopting a highway in your hometown.

## A Time and Season for Everything

Your own life circumstances will do much to determine where and how you can serve.

Consider this example: A young mother rushed into the office of a local food bank, exclaiming. "It's taken me months to finally find a baby-sitter and get down here to help. What can I do?"

"Go home," the director said gently. "Wait until your children are grown up a bit. They are the ones who need your help the most now."

Recognizing limitations that might hold you back now is important. After all, limitations usually change with time—one day you really might have time to work at that homeless shelter.

A helping attitude doesn't go away during different stages in life, but its direction will vary from year to year:

• Children who learn to help alongside adults may finish projects their leaders don't have time to complete. Dad and Mom may plant the garden, but even young kids can water and weed it.

• Youth tend to help with energy and enthusiasm when they care about a cause. This makes them good organizers as well as dedicated participants in planned projects.

• Young adults and college students possess skills that qualify them to help in a variety of areas. Most college students are eager to use their newly acquired training and explore new frontiers.

• Professionals in the work force are the backbone of mentoring programs for youth and adults. Mentoring another individual takes only a few hours a week and can be squeezed into lunch hours, evenings, or weekends.

• Parents of growing children can direct their energy to helping with their children's activities in local schools or on athletic teams. Volunteering to be a little league coach simultaneously helps your own child and others'.

• As their children grow, many adults discover cravings to help at locations away from home or work. Doing so allows them to hone their own skills or develop new talents.

• Retired adults can use a lifetime of experience and newfound free time to volunteer full-time alongside professionals, or to serve in more low-key positions a few hours a week.

## VOLUNTEER RIGHTS

As you begin volunteering your time in areas large and small, educate yourself about the area in which you choose to serve. Finding the right volunteer position is remarkably similar to looking for the right job. Anticipate the application process— interviews, tours, introductions—as an opportunity to investigate your options. Because you don't have to worry about bringing in a paycheck, you can be more selective with the volunteer positions you accept. Volunteers have rights. They also have responsibilities. Be aware of them. They will help you know what questions to ask, what information to give about yourself, and what level of commitment to undertake. Consider the following:

• To volunteer is a basic right. Everyone should have the opportunity to give help for the benefit of others.

• A volunteer has a right to know what is expected: amount of time, length of commitment, type of preparation. Then it becomes a volunteer's responsibility to fully keep commitments.

• A volunteer has a right to be treated as a unique person with special skills and interests. A volunteer is also obligated to work smoothly with coworkers to achieve the goals of the organization.

• A volunteer has a right to adequate training (taking into account previous learning and experience). A volunteer must be open to new learning, ideas, and insights.

• A volunteer has a right to participate in setting goals for service—sharing ownership of the experience with the organization.

• A volunteer has a right to receive satisfaction from the work—to feel it has real purpose—beyond personal gains. A volunteer must expect to receive evaluation and positive critique. (*The Volunteer Center Handbook* [Salt Lake City: The Volunteer Center, 2000], 6–7.)

## DECIDING WHERE TO SERVE

As you begin volunteering, think about the causes that are important to you:

• Consider the skills you have to offer or the new areas you would like to learn something about.

• Decide whether you want to work alone or with others.

• Look for helping opportunities that will reinforce your other goals in life.

• Don't be anxious about the application or interviewing process; it is in everyone's best interest to match you with a position you can fill well and enjoy.

• Look forward to training; it is one of the great opportunities of volunteering. The most sought after attitude is that of an eager learner.

• Expect requirements for many volunteer positions. Such requirements may include a background check, a driving record check, a TB test—depending on the population you are to serve.

• Laugh a little, smile a lot. One of the ten top tips for volunteering is to bring a sense of humor.

• Remember that at some point you will need to take a leap; service is an adventure.

## A WORD ON OVEREXTENDING

The perfect combination of rights and responsibilities is what every volunteer is looking for, and that balance is individual. Don't overestimate the time and energy you can schedule for serving others. What you hope to do and can do must be realistically evaluated or you may become a disappointment to an organization rather than a help.

If you plan to volunteer for a organized group or program, don't forget that there will be times when your child may get sick, your neighbor may need your support, or your professional deadlines may demand that you stay on the job. In some programs, dependability is critical above all else. Look for flexible types of service that may be more suitable to your current situation.

## SERVING AS A FAMILY, A NEIGHBORHOOD, A COMMUNITY, AND BEYOND

Service occurs at all levels of society. As you consider where your skills will be best put to use, look at the people and world around you. Does one of your children need a reading tutor?

Could your family serve together by helping a neighbor in need? Would you and your spouse be able to make changes in your own community, or do you have ideas that could extend to neighboring communities and regions? Do your employees or coworkers have the time and means to give back to the community by implementing improvement initiatives or cleanup projects? The ways you can serve really are endless.

### In the Home

Service is learned best in families. The critical lessons that teach young people how to live a productive and happy adult life are grounded in caring for those around them. Parents provide a service to their children simply by embracing learning as an enduring aspect of life, teaching the value of work by doing it, and teaching social and practical skills. In the family, children can learn to communicate effectively, to understand differences, to respect others, and to manage resources.

An ideal setting for family growth occurs when adults and children learn lessons simultaneously. Concurrent growth gives off powerful bonding energy. Finding a service opportunity can be a joint exploration and application of family values. Families can serve in most ways one would think to serve individually. If you want to implement a lifelong tradition of family service, begin by considering your family's assets, which include:

• The ages and skills of family members

• The times people are available (after school, Saturday mornings)

• The location of involvement (in your own home or away)

• Your children's hobbies and talents

• The materials on hand (craft supplies, building supplies, camping gear, a computer)

• The possibility of team participation (parent with child, older sibling with younger sibling)

• The advantage of serving with extended family (grandparents, aunts, uncles, cousins)

As your family begins serving one another and serving together, you will quickly discover the rewards of service and the difference that can be made in the lives of those you love most. Here are just a few of the results your own family may recognize:

• More quality time together

• The joy of sharing a common purpose

• Learned self-confidence and increased skills

• An enlarged circle of friends, including people from different backgrounds and circumstances

### In the Neighborhood

L. J. Hanifan, an early twentieth-century reformer, wrote that "The individual will find in his associations the advantages of the help, the sympathy, and the fellowship of his neighbors."

When you serve your neighbor, you are really serving the neighborhood. Neighborliness tends to spread itself around, creating friendships and associations that build confidence and trust. Once trust is built, neighbors can begin serving together and strengthening the homes and streets on which they live.

In his book *Bowling Alone*, author and Harvard professor Robert D. Putnam explores the negative effects of neighborhoods and societies which do not foster a sense of community. We used to go bowling in leagues, he explains, but modern times have shaped us into people who go "bowling alone," or in small informal groups, and don't take advantage of the unity and trust that comes from joining together as neighbors and associates. He believes that when trust becomes a neighborhood value, people are not only happier but they also live longer and give back more to society (see Robert Putnam, *Bowling Alone: The Collapse and Revival of American Community* [New York: Simon & Schuster, 2000], 134–47). According to Putnam, people who trust their fellow citizens:

- Volunteer more often

- Contribute more to charity

- Participate more often in politics and community organizations

- Serve more readily on juries

- Give blood more frequently

- Comply more fully with their tax obligations

- Are more tolerant of minority views

- Display many other forms of civic virtue (ibid., 136–37)

Different types of neighborhood groups can have substantially different impacts on the cohesiveness of the vicinity. Neighborhoods are strengthened if service to local organizations, such as churches, study groups, and clubs—which are exclusive by definition—are balanced with service to neighborhood programs, such as youth service groups (Boy Scouts, Girl Scouts, 4–H), schools, and local recreation programs which include everyone.

Neighbors who know each other tend to care about each other. The more connections, the stronger the neighborhood. Good neighbors can serve by:

- Offering mutual support

- Becoming a network of contacts when someone is seeking a new job

- Assisting those who are hurt or in danger

- Expediting neighborhood improvements

- Noticing and resolving neighborhood problems

- Working to improve the quality of the local schools

- Enhancing the safety of the area

- Organizing social/service interaction, such as street parties and holiday service projects

### In the Community

Communities extend beyond the few streets and blocks that surround your own home. They encompass hospitals, fire stations, parks, care centers, churches, and many other entities that need your help to better serve those who live in the area. All over this country are hundreds of social service and nonprofit organizations whose purposes are two-fold:

1. To serve people and communities in need

2. To create opportunities for people to experience the joy of serving others

If you want to volunteer in an organized setting and directly influence your own community, start by finding the agencies and organizations that serve people in your community:

• Check the phone book under Social Service Agencies or Human Services.

• Check the local newspaper for a "Volunteer Corner." This is usually a weekend feature.

• Call the local Volunteer Center. (Five hundred exist in one or more locations in all but a few states. They link individuals, families, students, businesses, civic, community, and faith-based organizations with places or issues where their service can be utilized effectively.)

• Find out if a "Community Collaborative" exists in your area. Collaboratives are made up of groups like hospitals, food banks, social services, and faith-based groups, as well as nonprofit organizations that hold regular meetings to communicate and coordinate service.

• Check local government listings for volunteer opportunities.

• Call hospitals, schools, museums, and other locations that use volunteers or docents.

• Ask your employer about work-related volunteer opportunities.

• Join a formal service organization.

• Ask around about smaller charitable organizations or support groups of special interest.

• Look at the Web sites on the Internet that list community volunteer opportunities. These sites are designed for searches by location (your state and zip code), areas of interest, and the distance from home you are able to travel. They list possible volunteer service in areas such as the arts, education, the environment, health, human services, and religion.

## Beyond

Just as service unites communities, it can also unite a nation. When a national disaster strikes, people from all over the country rush to help. Organ, blood, and human milk donations are shared throughout the nation. Relief organizations collect supplies from citizens in the United States to send abroad.

Unity is the urgent goal of a country in peril but is often harder to achieve in prosperous times. A strong democracy must find bipartisan causes to rally around and support with service. You can help by simply doing the following:

• Fly the American flag on national patriotic holidays such as Martin Luther King Jr. Day, Presidents' Day, Memorial Day, Independence Day, Veterans Day—even Flag Day and Election Day.

• Follow national issues and candidates; write letters to congressmen or the newspaper.

• Vote; serve as an electoral judge.

• Support the Points of Light Foundation which, along with its 500 volunteer centers across the country, sponsors *Seasons of Service*—five national days of service each year (Martin Luther King Jr. Service Day in January, National Youth Service Day in April, Join Hands Day in June, Make a Difference Day in October, and National Family Volunteer Day in November).

• Share the goal of America's Promise—The Alliance for Youth, which is committed "to mobilize people from every sector of American life to build the character and competence of our nation's youth."

Beyond patriotism and concern for our nation's well-being is cultural understanding and empathy for other peoples of the world. Serving those beyond our borders is a meaningful way to volunteer your time and talents. The prerequisite to effective helping in the world is understanding. The disparities in the world may undermine our effectiveness if we somehow think our way of doing things is surely best. Native villagers, for example, may feel resistance to change if developmental plans depend solely on imported ideas, supplies, and supervisors. Liz Nolan, a participant in an international living program, traveled to Kenya and found that her service came in the simple ways. "I spent a lot of time just working and cooking in the hut with my host mother. One morning when we were sitting together quietly, she said, 'God has blessed me so much, because he has brought us together. And I am so happy.' She lived in a poor farming community yet she had everything she could want" (in *World Odyssey* [Brattleboro, Vt.: World Learning, 2001], 28).

Much has been learned as Americans have started helping others throughout the world. But even assisting villagers in obtaining sufficient food and clean water must be done wisely in order to strengthen rather than frustrate community development. Keep in mind these three important details if you choose to serve in this way:

1. Work through an established organization to gain experience.

2. Establish a relationship with native people; work side by side.

3. Assure adequate training of local people to maintain and perpetuate projects.

As you begin, remember that the goal of world service organizations is to increase goodwill and empower other people to meet their own needs. Examples of world service organizations include:

• An international service organization that facilitates the training of local professionals in healthcare. The native trainees then serve thousands of others during their lifetime.

• A nonprofit organization that sponsors micro-credit loans to the very poor based on principles of discipline, unity, courage, and hard work. Sponsors and recipients attend weekly meetings together where they answer questions, dispense low-interest loans, pay interest, and share stories.

• A faith-based organization that offers an advance on tuition and expenses for technical training to young adult applicants in developing countries. Based on principles of self-reliance, the participants pay back the loans (with minimal interest) when they have employment, perpetuating assistance to others.

• A sister city organization that develops a school curriculum about its foreign city. Elementary school students in the United States send maps, favorite storybooks, and class photos; students there send back crafts, traditional stories, and accounts of how their city is progressing.

## HOW TO USE THIS BOOK

Whether you want to make a difference in the world or in your own home, this book will help you get started. The following pages are full of ideas that will connect you to service opportunities and volunteer experiences in areas such as animal care, childhood literacy, healthcare, sports, and technology. More than one thousand ideas in twenty-six different areas are included. Browse through these pages and find an area that interests you. Each chapter begins with a simple list of things that everyone can do in that area to make a difference. The chapter then goes into detail about specific volunteer opportunities in that area: organizations you can join, Web sites to visit, training, and so on.

The following symbols will help you navigate the book efficiently:

● **Groups.** Although anyone can take on these ideas, they are especially appropriate for youth and adult groups, such as company employees, Sunday school classes, or service organizations who want the experience of serving as a team.

♥ **Families.** While anyone can perform these acts of service, they are particularly well suited for families and will help your family develop a sense of unity as you work together. Families with both young and grown children can carry out these ideas.

★ **Youth.** Many organizations can utilize the services of youth as young as twelve, others have programs for fourteen to sixteen year olds. Youth seeking to serve for experience or to fill school assignments will find these ideas particularly helpful.

♥ **Professional Qualifications.** These volunteer positions require professional training, such as a medical degree, therapy expertise, or a teaching certificate.

⚡ **Training Required:** These areas of service may require training that will be provided by the organization, such as literacy training, first-aid certification, and so on.

## Going Online

Now that you're ready to begin, check out these Web sites for helpful information on volunteering:

www.americaspromise.org
www.nationalservice.org (Corporation for National and Community Service)
www.networkforgood.org (formerly www.helping.org)
www.pointsoflight.org
www.volunteerconnections.org (Volunteer Center National Network)
www.volunteermatch.org

## A Few Notes

• Information throughout this book is subject to change: organizations move, Web sites change names or shut down during redesigns, and so on. If the organization you are looking for is no longer at the address given, a simple search in the Internet—

based on the organization's name—will usually supply the most current information.

• Keep in mind that Internet resources and organizations contained in this book are not exhaustive; they are simply representative of the great variety of helpful resources online.

• The telephone dialing code 211 can be used in nine states— and will soon be available in nearly every other state—to access nationwide health and human services information free of charge. This tool could be helpful to you as you work to serve others and make a difference.

# ANIMALS

*Animal envoys still must sleep, somehow, within us; for they wake a little and stir when we venture into wilderness.*

*–Joseph Campbell*

The wildlife habitats you visit and enjoy today are the same places your children—and their children—will enjoy in the future. Likewise, they are the same areas that generations of animal life have called and will continue to call home for years to come. Because we already share the world

| | |
|---|---|
| ● | Groups |
| ♥ | Families |
| ★ | Youth |
| ♥ | Professional Qualifications |
| ⚑ | Training Required |

with animals, it helps significantly to consciously preserve their habitats. Here are some things that everyone can do to make a difference:

> *Observe nature but leave it undisturbed.*
>
> *Obey hunting and fishing regulations and encourage others to do so.*
>
> *Don't feed wildlife or leave food accessible.*
>
> *Carry out of protected areas what you carry in; pick up after others.*

## GOVERNMENT WILDLIFE SERVICES

The United States Fish and Wildlife Service is assisted by thousands of volunteers each year. Working side-by-side with Wildlife Service employees, volunteers can help with activities such as:

15

- Bird banding
- Habitat restoration
- Conducting wildlife population surveys
- Trail building
- Staffing visitor centers and leading tours
- Performing clerical or computer assistance in Service offices
- Photographing natural resources

To watch after national wildlife refuges in individual communities, the U.S. Fish and Wildlife Service depends on National Wildlife Refuge Support Groups, called "Friends." Those affiliated with "Friends" are private citizens who join other volunteers to help with:

- Organized cleanups ★ ⚥
- Construction of viewing platforms and duck blinds
- Distribution of information to the public
- Research and project planning ❦
- Special events, such as National Wildlife Refuge System Week, International Migratory Bird Day, National Public Lands Day ● ♥ ★

Seven regional offices of the U.S. Fish and Wildlife Service exist throughout the country. Each has a volunteer coordinator who can direct people to the needs in their region. State governments also have their own divisions of wildlife resources, with individual agendas and field offices. A state division, for example, may train mentors to teach children about fish and aquatic resources in an urban area.

## BIRDS

Aviaries throughout the United States have programs that utilize the services of volunteers. The more hours volunteers log, the more privileges they gain for working directly with the birds. Volunteers learn to:

- Clear out exhibits. ★ ⚥
- Prepare birds' special diets. ★ ⚥
- Clean birds' beaks and nails. ★ ⚥
- Assist with bird shows. ★ ⚥

Non-profit rehabilitation organizations for wildlife are also spread throughout the country and are always looking for assistance. Local rehabers may assist aviaries (where injured birds are often taken) on their own time and expense. They care for birds, including birds of prey, until they can safely return to nature. Opportunities are available for:

> *Cleaning out the mews has its benefits. It's not just dirty work, because it gives the birds a chance to get acquainted with who you are. Once you've cleaned their area for a while they become much more comfortable perching on your hand. When you work with birds you build relationships.*
>
> *—Jennifer Hagg, Volunteer Coordinator at Tracy Aviary*

- Hen raising ♥
- Care of injured birds ⚥
- Distribution of information to businesses, schools, and libraries

## ZOOS

Running a zoo is very costly, so volunteers are sought to serve as ambassadors of the zoo's mission. Volunteers learn to educate people of all ages in everything from butterflies to bears. Helping at a zoo is a training and teaching opportunity. Training typically includes learning about animal and wildlife conservation as well as a wide variety of animals. Volunteers can receive extensive handling instruction on animals such as ferrets, parrots, snakes, lizards, and invertebrates. They may also receive training on responsible animal care (preparation of diets, animal observation, and so on) and bio-facts (animal artifacts).

Docents and volunteers at zoos usually purchase their own manuals, badges or uniforms as required, and pay appropriate dues and enrollment fees. Docents and volunteers must also submit verification of an annual tuberculosis skin test. Zoos have a variety of programs, which may include training to become:

- Docents, who educate zoo visitors and lead tours through different areas of the zoo (50 hours of training plus additional hours to maintain animal handling status, are generally required.) ⚚

- Zoo aides, who assist with animal care and special events ★ ⚚

- Zoo interpreters, who assist with on-site education and must work at least one day a week in the summer and one day a month in the winter to remain qualified ★ ⚚

- Junior zoo keepers, who help clean enclosures, assist with animal diets, and maintain zoo areas for one shift a week in the summer ★ ⚚

## Animal Shelters, Community Farms, and Ability Camps

Abandoned and orphaned animals are everywhere. You can help local animal shelters and other organizations involved with animal care in many ways:

- Adopt an animal. ♥ ★

- Assist with super animal "adoptathons." ● ♥ ★

- Participate in community outreach education programs. ● ★

- Care for a too young, sick, or injured animal until it becomes adoptable. ♥ ★

The Humane Society or other animal shelter in your community will likely appreciate assistance from volunteers who can:

- Follow up with people who have recently adopted a pet—give suggestions on behavioral problems.

- Provide care for shelter animals—filling water bowls, walking and playing with animals, and so on (be aware that most shelters will want your help cleaning up animal refuse as well). ★
- Welcome shelter visitors; match pet requests with waiting animals.
- Transport animals between sites.
- Provide clerical support; expedite the return of pet licenses to customers.

Community farms and ability camps (recreation centers for people with disabilities to interact with animals)—or anywhere animals receive daily care—appreciate volunteer help. Most community farms and ability camps do worry about training volunteers who won't end up assisting enough to be worth the time and effort needed to train them. Accept training only if you are committed to staying on and helping for a reasonable period of time. If you choose to help in this area, you may be asked to:

- Feed animals. ★ ⚲
- Groom animals. ★ ⚲
- Help clean enclosures. ★ ⚲

## PET THERAPY

Programs are available in many communities where people and their pets or other available animals are teamed and then screened, trained, and certified to perform Animal-Assisted Therapy. Pet therapy involves taking your pet on visits to patients or residents of hospitals or care centers. People can be paired with dogs and cats, as well as birds, rabbits, goats, domesticated rats, hamsters, guinea pigs, ducks and chickens, and miniature pigs (llamas, cows, and horses are used in farm-like settings), all of which make wonderful visiting animals and may form strong human-animal bonds.

Animals that do well in giving pet therapy are usually social and predictable. Most should have the ability to walk on varied surfaces. The qualities of those who want a pet partner are equally important. If you're interested in this type of volunteer work, ask yourself the following questions:

1. Do you relate comfortably with your animal?

2. Are you willing to receive training?

3. How do you correct your dog in public?

---

*As I pulled into the parking lot with my Doberman, Marz, I had mixed feelings of anticipation and apprehension about our new assignment. I had been told that Joey, the child we were about to see, had been severely abused and refused to talk about what had been done to him by the adults he trusted and loved. . . . When we entered the room, Joey looked us over but said nothing. He paid no attention to the therapist but soon began to interact with Marz. . . . Our visit the following week had most unexpected results. . . . Joey asked his therapist to leave the room. He asked me to go around the corner. . . . I soon heard him talking to Marz. I peeked around the corner and saw Joey sitting with his arm around my dog, pouring out his heart.*

—Peggi Nash, Pet Partner

---

Teams who become registered are then eligible to participate in any number of volunteer programs, where they render valuable emotional service to young and old. You and your pet may be asked to:

- Participate with patients in hospitals. ♥ ⚡
- Visit residents in care facilities. ♥ ⚡
- Assist therapists with treatment of challenging children. ♥ ⚡
- Support victims of disasters. ⚡

## PUPPY RAISING PROGRAMS

Trained dogs are needed to assist not only people with blindness but people with many other physical and developmental disabilities. A highly trained dog may respond to more than fifty specialized commands and become the physical extension of its partner by performing a variety of tasks, such as turning off a light switch for a person in a wheelchair or alerting someone who is deaf to a fire alarm. People who love dogs and want to assist people with disabilities can:

- Care for a pedigreed puppy that is eight weeks to somewhere between thirteen and eighteen months old. ♥
- Provide indoor living accommodations, crate training, day supervision, or veterinary services. ♥
- Teach house training and basic obedience skills. ♥ ⚥
- Attend approved training classes. ⚥
- Pick up and return puppy upon request.

## MORE IDEAS FOR EXPANDING SERVICE

For further service opportunities involving animals, you may want to look into something similar to one of these unique programs:

- One non-profit organization in Chicago sponsors a youth enterprise dedicated to helping at-risk youth have experience with animals, enjoy pets, and develop skills. Inner-city youth tend and care for goats. The goat milk is made into cheese and sold by the youth to restaurants and specialty food stores (for more information, see Warren Cohen, "Chicago Garden Project Grows Budding Entrepreneurs," *World Ark* [Urban Agriculture: Helping Kids Survive the City], Summer 2000, 2–4). ● ★ ⚥
- Other urban youth in Chicago are learning how to raise fish and worms. The fish are raised in an indoor aquaculture system made of fifty-five-gallon drums. Fingerlings help supplement the daily diet in neighborhoods where 90 percent of the people live on welfare. They are also profitable for youth to market. The worms' castings make excellent fertilizer (see ibid., for more information). ● ★ ⚥

## Suggested Reading

Mary Burch, *Volunteering with Your Pet: How to Get Involved in Animal-Assisted Therapy with Any Kind of Pet*, New York: Howell Book House, 1996.

## Internet Resources

Search Animal Shelters>state
www.netpets.org

## Organizations

In addition to local animal shelters and state or regional fish and game offices, try contacting one of the following:

Canine Companion (regional centers are located in California, Colorado, Florida, Illinois, Minnesota, New York, and Ohio)
P. O. Box 446
2965 Dutton Ave.
Santa Rosa, CA 95402–0446
707–577–1700
www.caninecompanions.org

Delta Society (Pet Partners, Animal-Assisted Therapy)
580 Naches Ave. SW, Suite 101
Renton, WA 98055–2297
425–226–7357
www.deltasociety.org

Guide Dogs of America
13445 Glenoaks Blvd.
Sylmar, CA 91342
818–362–5834
www.guidedogsofamerica.org

Intermountain Therapy Animals (largest affiliate of Delta Society)
P. O. 17201
4835 S. Highland Dr. Space 2125
Salt Lake City, UT 84117
801–272–3439
www.therapyanimals.org

Therapy Dogs International, Inc.
88 Bartley Rd.
Flanders, NJ 07836
973–252–9800
www.tdi-dog.org

United States Fish & Wildlife Service
1849 C St., NW
Washington D.C. 22040
202–208–5634
www.fws.gov
Regional offices http://offices.fws.gov

# ARTS: DANCE, DRAMA, MUSIC, AND VISUAL ARTS

*Talent is long patience.*
—Gustave Flaubert

Art beautifies everything around it, inspires those who participate in it, and spawns creativity. Both the young and the old benefit from exposure to cultural, visual, and fine art.

| | |
|---|---|
| ● | Groups |
| ♥ | Families |
| ★ | Youth |
| ♦ | Professional Qualifications |
| ☂ | Training Required |

Art programs also teach important skills such as perception, critical thinking, and empathy. In fact, college entrance examination results show that students who participate in the arts score nearly one hundred points higher on the SAT than students who don't (see www.vsarts.org/info/faq.html). But there are thousands of children with parents who don't care or can't afford to pay the price for their children's early arts education. Individuals and communities may try to compensate. Everyone can make a difference by:

Attending recitals, concerts, and exhibits. Be the audience for children and youth.

Providing performance opportunities for young musicians, dancers, and actors.

Taking children to story hours and puppet shows and encouraging them to improvise by creating their own productions.

*Making available safe chaperoned venues for youth dances.*

*Sponsoring cultural programs where ethnic groups share their unique music, dance, and art.*

*Telling children stories; passing on an oral tradition of your cultural heritage.*

*Offering young people good music for listening and learning; playing it at home as well.*

*Protecting yourself and others from loud piercing music. (Just because it's "music" won't save someone from sound-induced hearing loss.)*

*Displaying art at home and at work. Include work by children and youth.*

*Inviting older neighbors without transportation and people with disabilities to attend performances.*

## DANCE

Dance is a powerful medium for teaching discipline. Along with ballet and creative dance, elements of break dancing and hip-hop can be taught to entice youth into dedicating themselves to dance performance.

- Dance studios can allow at-risk youth to participate in programs on "scholarship" if they can't pay for their lessons. Studios may also allow kids from low-income families to "pay" for lessons by doing minimal janitorial work in the studio. Participants in programs such as this must be willing to meet specific criteria (i.e., no drugs, stealing, bar hopping, etc.), attend scheduled practices (often daily) and extra rehearsals in preparation for performances. ♥

Dancers can participate in a variety of programs that help youth, children, and the elderly to experience the invigoration and fulfillment that comes from dancing and exercise. Dancers who have studied dance therapy in university or college programs are particularly well suited for this type of volunteer work. But

> *They're dancing for their lives. That's why they have that energy. They hope they can be something. They've figured out that the drug of being on stage is much more powerful than the drug of marijuana. They tell me, "We've found the high here."*
>
> —*Adriano Welch, director of a dance program for at-risk kids*

high school dancers may also find opportunities to serve through dance. You may want to contact Dance Adapt, a national in-service and pre-service teacher-training program that works to involve children with disabilities in their school's curricula and community events (www.vsarts.org/programs/index. html). Sponsors of dance programs should provide music and lead the way for organizing successful programs. Here are some ways dancers can volunteer:

- Teach after-school classes to children at inner-city elementary schools. ● ★
- Participate in hospital rehabilitation programs. ♥
- Teach dance classes for young people with disabilities. ♥
- Lead dance therapy sessions in senior centers/nursing homes. ♥

## DRAMA

Acting is a healthy outlet for pent-up emotions. Neglected or abused children benefit from "acting out" their fears and frustrations. Whether in the audience or on stage, people can vicariously experience life traumas and ecstasies as a relief from personal stress. Those who volunteer to help theater companies and directors of school plays (all notoriously on tight budgets) are providing a service to the community. During the preparation of a production, organizers are always looking for volunteers to:

- Build sets. ●
- Paint and dress sets. ● ♥ ★
- Collect props. ● ♥
- Sew costumes. ● ♥

- Hang posters. ● ♥ ★
- Usher.

## MUSIC

The power music has over listeners has made it a popular tool for therapy. And music—from classical to rock—is one of the highest forms of entertainment. Music lovers are usually passionate about affording to others what brings them delight. The ways to help are infinite:

> Music, the human voice, and language—it's the perfect combination. I see it every week. Our choir members come to practice stressed out and exhausted. They don't know if they can even make it through the rehearsal. And after two hours of singing they are totally energized and refreshed. They "pay for the privilege" we like to say.
>
> —Jim Kennard, manager of the Eleanor Kennard Chorale

- Teach young people to play, to sing, and to appreciate good music. If the children in your neighborhood are receiving plenty of assistance, venture out to help with a music program in a low-income area.

- Join a musical group—a choir or an orchestra. Practicing is inspiring and will uplift others. ♥ ★

- Entertain the lonely or sick with good music. Sing along or bring a tape player. Lend a music tape or share tapes borrowed from the library. ● ♥ ★

- Learn about the healing effects of music. Music therapy is an effective means of enabling people with traumatic backgrounds and disabilities. It is also helpful in easing pain and comforting the dying. ● ♥ ♥ ⚹

## VISUAL ARTS

The medium for visual art is limited only by imagination. Service with art can be focused on private expression or group participation. For example:

- Medical students, nurses, and hospital volunteers may work alongside pediatric patients as well as adults on projects that build trust and encourage talk about their shared hospital experience. ★

- Community youth may join with neighbors and artist mentors to create a mural on a building to beautify and increase respect in the neighborhood. ● ♥ ★ ❀

- City art organizations may commission a photographic history or the creation of a film documenting a new community building under construction or an old historic site scheduled for restoration or demolition. ●

- Mentor artists may offer art workshops or simply facilitate learning among art students. ❀

- Professional artists may volunteer to teach art enrichment units at public schools. ❀

- Adults who simply love art can become "art buddy" volunteers to youth.

---

*The man was struggling, frightened, unable to breathe. No more respirators, dilators, tracheotomies or medicines could resolve his disintegrated lungs. I held his frail body . . . but soon began leaning down to his left ear and singing Gregorian chant almost pianissimo. The chants seemed to bring him balance, dissolving fears, and compensating for those issues still full of sting.*

*—Therese Schroeder-Sheker, Founder of Chalise of Repose, a harp and voice assisted end-of-life patient care program*

---

## MUSEUMS

Visual art has captivated scholars and the public through the ages. Exposure to fine art is a gift available to the artist and novice alike. The selection of volunteers for a museum is based mostly on enthusiasm and commitment. Extensive training is required for docents (professionally trained volunteers) so that they can answer questions about art history and technique from adults and learn to ask intriguing questions of school-age children who visit the museum. Types of museum volunteer positions may include:

> *Every child is an artist. The problem is how to remain an artist once he grows up.*
>
> —*Pablo Picasso*

- Staffing information desks or gift shops ⚡
- Assisting with collection management, updating and maintaining artist and object files (may include research) ⚡
- Presenting community programs offsite, such as slide-illustrated lectures and hands-on workshops ⚡
- Acting as a tour guide (Special training for children, youth, and people with physical, emotional, sensory, and developmental disabilities may be provided.) ⚡
- Hosting foreign language-assisted tours ⚡
- Volunteering in a children's museum by assisting in creative projects or reading storybooks ★ ⚡

## COMBINED ARTS PROGRAMS

Town halls and community centers are hubs of entertainment, education, and artful display. Cities and towns may organize music shows, art displays, and classes—for children, youth, and adults alike—in subjects ranging from cartooning to culinary arts. Connecting with a cultural center provides many opportunities to give service, particularly with events. Volunteers can assist with:

- Changing exhibits ●
- Preparing for musical shows/plays ● ♥
- Hosting/ushering for events

Skilled artisans can also come up with unique ways of helping in the community:

- Potters may gather to donate bowls for a community soup dinner before a pottery fair.

- Film artists may assist youth in preparing for teen film festivals.

- Sculptors may build sand sculptures at the state fair or ice sculptures at the community's winter festival.

- Artists, composers, playwrights, and directors may share their talents in workshops during career development festivals.

## More Ideas for Expanding Service

Artists and other groups sponsor a variety of projects that involve volunteers and work to serve people throughout the community. Coming Up Taller, a division of the President's Committee on the Arts, sponsors hundreds of after-school, summer, and weekend arts programs throughout the United States (see www.cominguptaller. org/profile.html for specific details). Here is a sampling of the programs you could become involved in:

> *I didn't need punishment, I needed transformation. Art saved my life.*
>
> *—Patricia McConnel, ex-convict and participant in Heartland Collaborations, Iowa*

- Teens may be trained to go "on assignment" to photograph festivals and other community events or create personal photo essays to combat the negative portrayal of urban teens in the media. At the summer's end they may practice public speaking skills by presenting their photographed work to family, friends, and funders. (For more details, contact the Boston Photo Collaborative at 67 Brookside Avenue, Jamaica Plain, MA, 02130. 617–524–7729.)

- At the Indianapolis Museum of Art, youth are supervised in their study of art, architecture, history, or culture. The youth then prepare presentations, including lectures, displays, and hands-on activities, that they can take "on the road" to libraries, schools, and community centers. (For more details, contact the Indianapolis Museum of Art at 4000 N. Michigan Rd., Indianapolis, IN, 46208–3326. 317–923–1331.)

- In some regions, art education programs have been instigated to help students beautify their schools. Students have created dramatic art projects by designing and painting cast-concrete sculptured benches, large totem poles, and life-sized mixed-media puppets of people who have influenced history. (For more information, contact the Center for Development and Learning at 208 S. Tyler St., Suite A, Covington, LA 70433. 985–893–7777.)

- Many communities are creating original musical theater productions, which are used to apply conflict-resolution training in troubled neighborhoods. Youth who participate in these productions learn about methods for solving conflicts as they create, rehearse, and perform real-life dramatic pieces in churches, community centers, and juvenile detention centers. (For more information, contact the Mind-Builders Creative Arts Co. at 3415 Olinville Ave., Bronx, NY, 10467. 718–652–6256.)

- Community music centers offer free instrumental training for elementary students in low-income areas (i.e., two hours after school, three days a week). Students who conscientiously participate in a program for two years are given their own instruments and often become the backbone of middle school bands and orchestras. (For more information, contact the music center at Cesar Chavez Elementary School at 1404 S. 40th St., San Diego, CA, 92113. 858–459–3724.)

- Multi-disciplinary arts organizations help low-income teen mothers and their children learn music, movement, literature, storytelling, and drama to foster their development. (For more information, contact Christina Cultural Arts Center, Inc. at 705 N. Market St., Wilmington, DE, 19801. 302–652–0101.)

## Internet Resources

Arts and Healing Network
www.artheals.org

Coming Up Taller: Arts and Humanities Programs for Children and
   Youth at Risk
www.cominguptaller.org

National Assembly of State Arts Agencies (spotlights a wide variety of
   community art projects)
www.nasaa-arts.org

## Organizations

Contact local art centers, theaters, and museums.

Boys and Girls Clubs, community recreation centers and care
centers need assistance with arts and crafts projects.

Americans for the Arts (arts awareness ideas for schools)
Washington Office
1000 Vermont Ave., NW, 12th Floor
Washington D.C. 20005
202-371-2830

New York Office
One E. 53rd St.
New York, NY 10022
212-223-2787
www.artsusa.org

Arts Education Partnership
One Massachusetts Ave., NW, Suite 700
Washington D.C. 20001-1431
202-326-8693
http://aep-arts.org

President's Committee on the Arts and the Humanities
1100 Pennsylvania Ave., NW, Suite 526
Washington D.C. 20506
202-682-5409
www.pcah.gov

VSA Arts (learning opportunities through the arts for people with disabilities; affiliates in 40 states and 83 other countries)
1300 Connecticut Ave., NW, Suite 700
Washington D.C. 20036
800-933-8721
www.vsarts.org

# CELEBRATIONS
# AND HOLIDAYS

*I love a parade, the tramping of feet, I love ev'ry beat I hear of a drum. . . .*
*When I hear a band I just want to stand and cheer as they come . . .*
—Ted Koehler

Celebrations punctuate our lives; through them we vent emotion, commemorate achievement, and measure progress. Perhaps the greatest accomplishment of any celebration, however, is the unity it promotes. All Americans can make a difference and promote unity as they:

- ● Groups
- ♥ Families
- ★ Youth
- ♥ Professional Qualifications
- ⚹ Training Required

*Learn about the ethnic and religious festivals of diverse neighbors and associates.*

*Attend ethnic celebrations of other groups when the general public is invited.*

*Acknowledge holidays of others with cordial "best wishes."*

*Support adaptation of a work schedule to accommodate others' beliefs.*

*Include people of other beliefs and traditions in cultural and religious celebrations when appropriate.*

## PARADES

Parades are supported by millions of Americans as well as by television networks, commercial sponsors, chambers of commerce, ethnic groups, and a host of other organizations. Parades build a community reputation for esthetic values, enhance cooperation between private enterprise and local governments, are inclusive and free (because of donated time and effort), and strengthen ethnic pride.

Civic or business groups may volunteer their whole organizations to assist in parade planning and preparation. Keep in mind, however, that parade volunteers become more valuable over time, which is why volunteers are encouraged to return year after year and why parade organizers try hard to maintain a volunteer work force that is loyal and enthusiastic. If you volunteer to help with a parade, you may want to consider serving on a parade committee. Keep in mind that work on most committees will involve some type of training and may even require that you have professional qualifications. Committee assignments are particularly good projects for groups to work on together. Here is a sampling of parade committees that accept volunteers:

- Community relations committee (committee members act as liaisons between organizers and the community) ⚔
- Planning and policy committees ⚔
- Float committee ⚔
- Bands committee ⚔
- Other committee units (for example, clowns, antique cars, Scout groups, equestrian acts, and so on) ⚔
- Manpower committee ⚔
- Programs/publicity committee ♥ ★ ⚔
- Legal and insurance committees ♥ ⚔
- Safety and security committees ♥ ⚔
- Parade lineup committee ⚔
- Starting-line committee ⚔
- Marshalling committee (members help to keep parade entries moving) ⚔

- Communications committee (members facilitate communications between front and back of parade) ⚊
- Dispersal committee (members are stationed at the end of the parade route to direct participants to locations where they can disband floats or other entries) ⚊

While hundreds of volunteers may be needed to run a parade, thousands are needed to participate. Volunteers can participate in or as:

- People on floats or on the street ● ♥ ★
- Military and ethnic bands ● ★
- Drill teams ● ★
- Riding clubs ● ★
- School bands ● ★
- Clowns (volunteers with fantastic personalities, spontaneous moves, and some training make particularly good clowns) ⚊

## FESTIVALS AND COMMUNITY HOLIDAYS

Festivals throughout the United States include an array of activities and celebrations, including folk art displays, children's activities, stage entertainment, commemorative services, and evening balls.

> The celebration will promote a spirit of love that includes people of all ethnic and cultural backgrounds, faiths and individual talents. They're looking for a wide variety of volunteers . . . for it will include a culture fest.
>
> —News coverage of the Days of '47 Parade, Utah

Whether the celebrations stem from civic, ethnic, or historic pride, the success of any festival depends on participation by a whole community of volunteers. There are many ways to help with festivals and similar celebrations such as candlelight tours and state and county fairs. Service may include:

- Setting up displays ● ♥
- Staffing booths

- Demonstrating arts
- Performing as musicians, dancers, storytellers, and so on ♥
- Assisting with sound amplification and recording ♥
- Setting up lighting and electrical connections ♥
- Acting as escorts or guides ● ♥
- Loaning costumes, heirlooms, or other ethnic paraphernalia
- Cleaning up or returning loaned equipment

Patriotic holidays and community holidays (such as Bunker Hill Day in Suffolk County, Massachusetts; Kamehameha Day in Hawaii; and Pioneer Day in Utah) have their own local traditions that depend on volunteers to assist not only with parades but also with memorial services, reenactments, concerts, pageants, art fairs, and races.

## Thanksgiving

Thanksgiving is one of America's best-loved and most widely celebrated holidays. The celebration prompts many companies, agencies, churches, and civic groups to join in service. Here are a few ideas:

- Collect frozen turkeys for food banks. ● ♥ ★
- Sponsor Thanksgiving dinners for the homeless (usually in advance of the official day). ●
- Deliver turkeys in food boxes to low-income families and home-bound seniors. ● ♥ ★
- Serve meals in shelters and food kitchens on Thanksgiving Day (neighbors may volunteer to give regular staff a day off). ● ♥ ★ ⚥
- Participate in Volunteers of America's program for cooking up traditional fare and distributing hot plates of food in outreach vans to people who live on the street. ⚥

- Transport food to shut-ins (volunteers "for the day" may be willing to cover the routes of regular Meals on Wheels volunteers). ● ♥ ★

> *At a Thanksgiving dinner for the homeless we can do much more than give them food; we can help them find a way out. Once we find out why they are struggling, we can put them in a long-term program to help them get ahead. It is wonderful. We never get tired of holiday work,*
>
> —Philip Arena, homeless mission worker, Salt Lake City Utah Mission

## CHRISTMAS

Mid-winter gift giving is a far older tradition than Christmas gift giving. People of goodwill, regardless of their beliefs, are generous during the holiday season. During the Christmas season two-thirds more than the normal amount of charity is given in volunteer hours and four times the amount in donated goods.

Here are some holiday tips for helping and some good advice for everyone who wants to make a difference:

*Even small gifts make a big difference.*

*Older people want visits more than presents. Don't just drop off a holiday treat; plan time to talk.*

*Some charities that appreciate used goods during the year prefer new clothes and toys at Christmastime to supply "no-cost holiday stores" for the needy.*

*Violent toys are not given to needy children. Too often these children have personally experienced violence, and the toys may be a reminder.*

*Gifts of food and clothing for people who have no idea about American holidays (i.e., refugees and immigrants) are still needed.*

*Interfaith cooperation blesses everyone. Some Jewish congregations take over the food preparation at local Christian-run soup kitchens on Christmas Day.*

*A couple of years ago we went to help with the YWCA's Christmas store. Too many volunteers were there—tripping over each other—so we asked, "What items do you need?" After a short tour, the answer became obvious: there was plenty of stuff for younger children but nothing for teens. Then we saw a huge pile of toys up on the stage. "Oh, those are violent toys. We'll have to deal with them later." That was the clue we needed. We started returning the violent toys to stores in exchange for CD players. We did that twice a week until Christmas. One day we exchanged toys for 36 CD players plus CDs.*

*—Bruce and Deanna Hammond, YWCA volunteers*

More help is needed during the holiday season than during other times of year; cold weather requires more clothing, more fuel, and more food. In addition to goods, it's the joy of the season people want to share— the music, lights, trees, stories, even shopping and wrapping presents. Because loneliness can be as painful as poverty, looking around the neighborhood for ways to bring cheer is a great way to begin.

The following is a list of holiday helping ideas to get you started:

- Host a neighborhood open house. If neighbors exchange gifts, consider pooling them instead to give to a community food bank or a no-cost Christmas store for people in need. ● ♥ ★

- Help people with disabilities or seniors living alone to decorate their homes. (Offer to take down the decorations after the holiday as well.) ● ♥ ★

- Assist with Christmas lights in community farms, historical sites, and city parks. (Offer to put away decorations after the holiday.) ● ♥ ★

- Prepare a holiday program to present at a care center; hold a dress rehearsal of the program for the elderly seniors in your neighborhood. ● ♥ ★

- Leave anonymous treats on the doorstep of someone who is alone (one tradition is to start twelve days before Christmas and continue daily until Christmas Eve), or compile for neighbors a collection of favorite holiday stories that can be read each day before Christmas. ● ♥ ★

- Adopt an individual or a family. Help provide Christmas for those in interfaith hospitality centers, children's centers, adolescent homes, corrections facilities, low-income senior programs, refugee programs, or transitional living centers for people with disabilities. Watch your local newspaper for Sub for Santa contact numbers. ● ♥ ★

- Create an angel tree for your organization (or for The Angel Tree organization, which is set up for children of prisoners), where individuals can select a removable tag that describes an article or two for a child in a needy family. The individuals then buy, wrap, and return for delivery the item listed on the tag. ● ♥ ★

- Shop with a disadvantaged child. Escort the child to select presents for himself and his family. ● ♥ ★

- Sort donations of food for food banks and no-cost Christmas stores. ● ♥ ★

- Wrap gifts for community centers and mental retardation agencies. ● ♥ ★

- Decorate and fill a food box for a needy family. ● ♥ ★

- Distribute food collected by agencies to low-income families and low-income seniors living in their homes. ● ♥ ★

- Deliver a Christmas dinner to homebound members of your community (can be arranged through Meals on Wheels). ● ♥ ★

- Join with a congregation to prepare Christmas dinner for residents of a detox center, a shelter, or an adolescent home. ● ♥ ★

- Take unused holiday candy, left over from Christmas or any holiday, to corrections centers or shelters. ● ♥ ★

## MORE IDEAS FOR EXPANDING SERVICE

People who choose to celebrate holidays with service throughout the year are making wonderful contributions. Take a look at the following projects:

- Martin Luther King Day is observed by many as a "day on" instead of a "day off," where diverse citizens join in community service and break down ethnic barriers by working together for a good cause. This activity is sponsored annually by the Points of Light Foundation. ● ♥ ★

- Many individuals choose to serve on smaller holidays. For example, some women gather the Saturday before Mother's Day to do a service project for less fortunate women and their children: sewing quilts, cleaning the home of an elderly person, entertaining at a rest home, and so on. ● ♥ ★

- Because so many volunteers are available during the holidays, many regular employees of volunteer organizations take a break during the holidays while temporary volunteers fill in. This helps the regular volunteers to temporarily shift their emphasis for a while and come back refreshed at the beginning of the new year to continue on in their volunteer capacity.

## Suggested Reading

Valerie Lagauskas, *Parades: How to Plan, Promote & Stage Them*, New York: Sterling Publishing Company, 1982.

## Organizations That Sponsor Holiday Help

Area Agencies on Aging (Eldercare Locator, 800–677–1116, www.eldercare.gov)

Angel Tree: A Ministry for Prison Fellowship (www.angeltree.org)

Arc, The (Advocates for the Rights of Citizens w/ Mental Retardation, www.thearc.org)

Boys and Girls Clubs (800–854–CLUB, www.bgca.org)

Boys and Girls Ranches and Clubs—Sub for Santa

Catholic Community Services—adopt a refugee and Good Samaritan
   programs (www.catholiccharitiesusa.org)
Children's centers—Sub for Santa
Christmas Box House International, The (www.thechristmasboxhouse.org)
Community service centers
Food banks
Foster care organizations—no-cost Christmas stores
Homeless shelters
International Rescue Committee—adopt a refugee family
   (www.theirc.org)
Make-a-Wish Foundation (www.wish.org)
Multi-cultural centers
National Interfaith Hospitality Network (www.nihn.org)
Odyssey House, Inc. (www.odysseyhouse.org), or other substance abuse
   centers
Salvation Army, The (www.salvationarmyusa.org)
Senior citizen housing centers
Transitional living centers—adopt a person with disabilities
United Way (www.unitedway.org)
Volunteers of America (www.voa.org)
Youth corrections facilities
Youth Services
YWCA—no-cost Christmas stores (www.ywca.org)

# CHILDREN

*Train up a child in the way he should go: and when he is old, he will not depart from it.*

—*Proverbs 22:6*

Children are young for a very short time, with much to learn that will affect their lifetimes. Everyone can make a difference in a child's life by:

| | |
|---|---|
| ● | Groups |
| ♥ | Families |
| ★ | Youth |
| ♥ | Professional Qualifications |
| ⚓ | Training Required |

*Helping children work toward worthwhile goals.*

*Being thoroughly honest so children learn trust.*

*Teaching children how to find answers to their questions.*

*Inspiring respect by managing anger and frustration; apologizing when you make mistakes.*

*Living with material restraint; don't give children everything they want.*

*Sharing with children how you feel when you serve others.*

*Providing a positive role model to children while teaching basic life skills.*

The fact that more than one in five children in the United States lives below the poverty line is a problem that deserves a lot of attention (see Margaret L. Andersen and Howard F. Taylor, *Sociology: Understanding a Diverse Society*, Belmont, Calif.: Wadsworth/Thomson Learning, 2002). Children who never trust that they will have food, comfort, and unconditional love are thwarted, not only in their progression toward a healthy independence but also in their ability to concentrate, interact socially, and develop physically.

## EMOTIONAL HELP

Numerous community child-care facilities have sprung up to help children while their parents work to earn a living. In addition to providing safety, caring agencies aim to supply a comfortable environment with adequate food and toys, a place to nap, and developmentally appropriate education. Child care for disadvantaged children is far more than "baby-sitting." Foremost, these children need consistent and unconditional love—a gift that requires a lot of help from caring people—far beyond what these organizations can afford to pay. Here are some ways volunteers can help in community child-care facilities or other places where children need love, learning, and attention:

- Read to children. ● ★
- Conduct playtime activities. ● ★
- Help children with arts and crafts projects. ● ★
- Organize recreational activities. ● ★
- Assist elementary school children with their homework. ● ★
- Interact with children by doing craft projects together or taking them swimming in the pool after school. ● ★
- Mentor children in prevention of substance abuse, tobacco abuse, domestic abuse, and preventable diseases. ⚡
- Work with difficult children ages up to eight years of age when their mothers are in treatment or unavailable. ⚡ ♥
- Work in therapy groups with emotionally and behaviorally challenged preschool children. ⚡ ♥
- Assist with care of children through age eleven in a crisis nursery (temporary childcare facility for emergency situations). ⚡

- Interact with children in day care while parents attend ESL classes, substance abuse classes, teen parenting classes, or recover in a battered women's shelter. ⚹

- Provide shelter homes for children for three to thirty days. ♥ ⚹

## Early Education

The biggest lesson society is learning from the controversial Head Start program of the 1970s is that it's not enough. Children need help early on and during the entire educational process. To be effective, education must be personal, especially for children with special challenges. Millions of American children are not learning English in their homes. Most communities offer a delightful assortment of teaching opportunities for adults who want to get involved and learn right alongside children. Consider one of the following possibilities:

- Teach English as a second language to young children. ⚹

- Lead a Cub Scout or a Girl Scout troop.

- Teach children in Sunday school.

- Be a mentor for your state's division of Wildlife Resources; teach children about fish and aquatic resources. ⚹

- Volunteer at a museum to teach selected topics to elementary grade student classes; teach school groups that come to visit their galleries. ⚹

- Be a volunteer guide at county and state offices; take elementary school students on tours around the government offices. A county or state office may also prepare a lesson on government for a volunteer teacher to take into the schools. ⚹

- Assist non-profit groups that work in foreign countries by presenting cultural lessons about their programs in the public schools. ● ⚹

- Develop animated programs that explore social problems to take into preschools, elementary schools, or Cub Scout den meetings. Subjects may include blindness, cerebral palsy, deafness, learning disabilities, Down's syndrome, or divorce, foster care, gangs, drugs, prejudice, and graffiti (see www.home.earthlink.net/~alslc/projects.htm for specific ideas used in one community branch of the National Assistance League—www.nal.org). ● ♥ ★

## PHYSICAL HELP

Adequate clothing is not only a physical need but also a legitimate social want; dressing America's children often involves a network of concerned people serving together. Children's service organizations welcome help in furnishing:

> A schoolteacher in Los Angeles, Ruth Ann Montgomery, saw children from one family coming to school on a rotating basis. She discovered that the children were taking turns coming to classes in order to share one set of clothes. She began gathering cast-off clothing from her friends and family. Operation School Bell is the result and has furnished 13,500 needy children with new clothes for school, including uniforms where required.
>
> —More information available from the National Assistance League

- Prenatal kits and "Welcome Baby" kits to low-income mothers ● ♥ ★

- Comforters and teddy bears for abused children ● ♥ ★

- Backpacks with toiletries, toys, and reading and writing materials for children moved quickly into foster care ● ♥ ★

Children who have life-limiting conditions also require substantial assistance. Caring for a child with considerable disabilities can put tremendous stress on a family. Those families need supportive friendships. Community nursing programs look for volunteers who are willing to:

- Provide respite care to the families of ill children.

- Read or just listen to a child.

- Assist with the activities of daily living.

Cheering up a child cheers up a family. Organizations such as the Make-a-Wish Foundation focus on helping children who have life-threatening conditions. Such foundations depend on help from volunteers who will:

- Befriend a child who has a life-threatening condition. ● ♥

- Work with the child to ascertain and plan his or her fondest wishes. ● ♥

- Seek in-kind goods and services to implement the wish. ● ♥

## More Ideas for Expanding Service

Parents who have grown up without good examples in their lives may not be able to help their children without help from others. Perhaps one of the best ways to help children in unstable homes is to make sure their parents are equipped with the necessary skills for the job. Several organizations have made parent education their goal. These organizations look for volunteers with professional experience or people with practical experience who are willing to be trained to teach parents and the general public about child protection issues:

- Head Start programs want volunteers to teach parents about their role as the primary educator of their children. ⚸

- Prevent Child Abuse groups train volunteers to conduct presentations on parent education. They may also utilize trained volunteers to speak to students and other agencies about recognizing and reporting child abuse. ⚸

- Family literacy groups may use volunteers to lead early childhood and parent education activities. ⚸

- Children's service societies look for parent advocate volunteers to teach and model parenting skills on a one-on-one basis by visiting another parent weekly and showing the parent how to deal with difficulties. Volunteers also give tips on positive discipline and communication. ✗

---

*Tips for Helping Children of Varying Ages*

*18 months: Vary activities. Nurture conversation. Help children to share. Hold when insecure.*

*2 years: Allow them to practice making choices. Redirect misbehavior. Show affection.*

*3 years: Sponsor activities requiring coordination and interaction with other children. Encourage self-sufficiency. Teach visually.*

*4 years: Encourage creative effort, kindness, patience, and politeness. Establish limits and express love.*

*5 years: Encourage physical activities, conversation, and questions. Give specific praise.*

*6 years: Allow decisions with limited choices. Praise honesty. Be patient; teach repentance—everyone makes mistakes.*

*7 years: Support high-energy activities. Ask thought-provoking questions. Allow them to practice making right choices. Encourage concern for others.*

*8 years: Provide appropriate heroes and help set realistic goals. Foster group interaction and cooperation. Praise good behavior; be patient with clumsiness, giggling, and squirming.*

*9 years: Provide activities that develop skills and good sportsmanship. Teach with information and facts; encourage memorization, reading, and writing.*

*10 to 11 years: Teach fairness, sensitivity, and kindness. Show interest in their activities. Recognize physical maturing; don't compare them with others. Facilitate service.*

---

## Suggested Reading

James Garbarino, *Raising Children in a Socially Toxic Environment*, San Francisco: Jossey-Bass, 1995.

Stacey Bess, *Nobody Don't Love Nobody: Lessons on Love from the School with No Name*, Carson City, NV: Gold Leaf Press, 1994.

## Organizations to Contact

Look in the white pages to contact local chapters of the following entities and organizations:

Alternative high schools (with teen mother programs)
Big Brothers, Big Sisters (www.bbbsa.org)
Boy Scouts (www.bsa.scouting.org)
Boys and Girls Clubs
Children's centers
Children's museums
Children's service agencies
Christmas Box House International, The (www.thechristmasboxhouse.org)
Community day-care centers
Community nursing services
County housing
County youth services
Division of Child and Family Services
Easter Seals (www.easter-seals.org)
Family support centers
Girl Scouts (www.girlscouts.org)
Hospital palliative care centers
Make-a-Wish Foundation (www.wish.org)
Mental health centers
Museums
National Assistance League (www.nal.org/chapters/search.cfm)
Prevent Child Abuse America
    (www.preventchildabuse.org/get_local/index.html)
Volunteers of America, Children and Youth (www.voa.org)
YMCA (www.ymca.net)
YWCA (www.ywca.org)

# CORRECTIONS AND PRISONS

*I was in prison, and ye came unto me.*
—Matthew 25:36

With rare exception, the people in correctional facilities eventually return to society either to make a contribution or cause problems. There are a variety of ways in which volunteers can serve prisoners and their families, but there are also a number of things everyone can do to make a difference so that fewer people break the law and enter the corrections system:

- Groups
- Families
- ★ Youth
- Professional Qualifications
- Training Required

> *Respect and obey the law and encourage others to do so.*
>
> *Stay alcohol and drug free.*
>
> *Lock your home and your car. Do all you can to discourage theft.*
>
> *Be kind to families with an incarcerated member.*

## OBJECTIVES OF CORRECTIONS VOLUNTEERS

Those who volunteer in correctional facilities typically serve to help inmates change their lifestyles, attach to strong moral values, rid themselves of addictions, learn interpersonal relationship skills, and develop job skills.

Correctional programs vary greatly from state to state and within states themselves. Large population areas may have large

> I was never very observant or knowledgeable before I came to the prison. Everything I know, I learned here. I have discovered great knowledge and inspiration. I finally found myself. I was lost in the world.
>
> —Inmate, New York's Sing Sing prison

volunteer programs, which enrich and diversify assistance within large facilities. Smaller jails in more rural areas may depend on whatever the people in the adjacent community can offer—a choir director who offers to start a jail choir, for example.

## TIPS FOR THOSE WHO WANT TO VOLUNTEER

Corrections programs are very complex. As you think about how you'd like to help, consider some of these lesser-known facts:

• Community service is a primary component of juvenile programs.

• Youth programs don't always include placement in a correctional facility. Offenders may be put on probation status (house arrest, supervision by probation officers, drug testing).

• Sharing personal information with prisoners is dangerous (60 percent of those paroled return to prison within one year); asking about their offenses is typically prohibited.

• Prisons often run work programs that utilize inmate labor to offset operating costs. They may also offer community service options to compliant inmates.

• Adult correctional facilities must maintain a clear-cut division between inmates and the community for safety reasons. Screening of volunteers includes consent to a thorough background check, driving record, and references. Personal interviews and training occur prior to placement.

## JUVENILE CORRECTIONS

More than thirty states across the United States are participating in an experimental program for teens that allows juvenile offenders a singular experience: the opportunity to be tried before a court of their peers. The offender and other youth fill the roles of defendant, juror, and attorney. Teens listen to the circumstances surrounding the offense then determine a consequence for the offender, such as community service, writing essays related to the infraction, completing counseling, enrolling in treatment or an educational program, apologizing to the victim, and participating as a juror in subsequent teen court cases.

Teen courts serve multiple functions—they hold youth offenders accountable, educate other youth, and help everyone involved to develop lifelong skills in addressing youth crime. Many are hopeful that the experiment will not only be found broadly successful but also extend throughout the country, allowing youth to have a first chance at helping each other.

Helping juveniles requires some understanding of adolescent behavior. There are a variety of ways to assist youth offenders:

> *Julio had gone to a maximum security youth prison at age thirteen for the shotgun shooting of another kid who was competing with him as a drug dealer for a bit of turf. . . . But unlike so many other boys, Julio used the opportunity of being exposed to the prison program to turn his life around, to learn to read, and eventually to parlay his high intelligence, strong will, and sense of divine intervention into a college scholarship that put him on the road to a career in social work.*
>
> —James Garbarino, Ph.D., author of Lost Boys: Why Our Sons Turn Violent and How We Can Save Them

- Offer projects to youth who need to complete community service hours as part of their sentence or commitment. Your business, for example may need help with mass mailings, gardening, cleanup, moving to a new location, construction, and so on. ●
- Assist juveniles in completing court-ordered community service. ●
- Mentor an offender one-on-one, even in a locked facility. ⚧
- Make quilts, treats, or birthday surprises for youth in corrections facilities. ● ♥ ★
- Give donations of suitable books and good magazines for youth. ● ♥ ★

- Facilitate creative expression of offenders; teach a talent—writing, art, drama, music—in a corrections facility. ☧

- Interact with offenders in a wide variety of activities and programs and serve as a role model to promote positive values, leadership, and character. ☧

- Help interview and assess clients with multiple DUI convictions. ☧

## ADULT PROGRAMS

"Citizen volunteers," who help on an ongoing basis, and student volunteers, who devote at least five hours a week for a semester, can do a lot to assist corrections facilities in helping offenders become self-sufficient, educated, and law abiding citizens. The caseload of prison workers is very high, so many correction facilities look for volunteers to help shoulder the load. Some knowledge of substance abuse, mental health, transient and criminal behavior, as well as good communication skills are needed. Most positions require at least a six-month commitment. They may include:

*Facts:*

- *Property crimes outnumber violent crimes 3 to 1.*
- *Most offenders do not have a high school diploma*
- *A third of offenders committed their offense under the influence of alcohol.*
- *Sixty percent of offenders used drugs in the month before their offense.*
- *A third of drug offenders sentenced to treatment programs end up in jail.*
- *Sixteen percent of inmates are mentally ill; most of those have been put on medications.*

- Academic and special education tutors ☧

- Skill trainers (for areas such as art, carpentry, drafting, and horticulture) ♥

- Group facilitators (to help with alcohol and drug education—AA & NA) ♥ ☧

- Art educators/therapists ♥ ☧

- Employment specialists and counselors (to provide assistance in finding meaningful employment) ⚐
- Parent education specialists ⚐
- Pet therapists ♥ ⚐
- Interpreters ⚐
- Chaplains and church service volunteers ⚐
- Operations volunteers (security, maintenance, food service) ⚐
- Research assistants (interviewing, data collection) ⚐
- Office workers (intake, archiving, data entry) ⚐
- Case aides (for mental health offenders, for multiple offense DUI offenders, for high-risk offenders returning to society who need help finding suitable housing and developing social and recreational skills in a drug- and alcohol-free environment) ⚐

## FAMILIES OF OFFENDERS

Research shows that the most important elements an individual needs to keep from returning to jail are a job and a strong family connection. Families of offenders need support to endure and to provide positive examples for their loved one in jail. The family that perpetuates hope in an incarcerated member is investing in the future. With strong family support, joined by good friends, an offender can often find a job even before release (which may be a condition of parole).

| Average Caseloads for Correctional Probation Officers in Florida 2000–2001 | |
| --- | --- |
| Community Control | 26.1 |
| Community Supervision | 77.1 |
| Sex Offender Supervision | 49.1 |
| Post-Prison Release Supervision | 49.1 |
| Drug Offender Probation | 47.1 |

(Statistics courtesy Florida Department of Corrections, Bureau of Statistics and Data Analysis)

Saving the families of offenders has become a movement of its own. There are organizations looking for people to help:

- Provide Christmas gifts for prisoners' children. ● ♥ ★

- Volunteer at summer camps for children of parents in prison.

- Help children visit a parent in prison.

- Facilitate virtual visiting (a radio station might provide an occasional broadcast where families and inmates can communicate, for example).

- Make jobs available for former prisoners (a tax credit is available for employers who do this). ●

- Provide refreshments for families visiting prisoners on the weekends. ● ♥ ★

## MORE IDEAS FOR EXPANDING SERVICE

Those who serve time in corrections facilities not only leave behind families but the victims of their crimes. The victims are sentenced to their own path of healing and forgiveness. Volunteers can help victims of crimes in many ways:

- Answer victim hotlines; listen while victims talk it out. ⚥

- Provide assistance at victims' homes—care for children, make phone calls, run errands. ⚥

- Join a local victim assistance program. ⚥

- Serve in crisis intervention, short-term emotional support, sexual assault examinations. ⚥

- Make assault kits (these usually contain toiletries). ● ♥ ★

- Collect and donate new clothing for assault survivors who many times must give their clothing to the police for evidence. ● ♥ ★

- Provide underwear and T-shirts to hospitals for low-income victims of accidents whose clothes must be cut off or turned over to police. ● ♥ ★

## Suggested Reading

Lois Wright and Cynthia Seymour, *Working with Children and Families Separated by Incarceration: A Handbook for Child Welfare Agencies,* Washington D.C.: CWLA Press, 2000.

## Internet Resources

The Corrections Connection
www.corrections.com

The Other Side of the Wall (writings on the impact of prison, including literary compositions)
www.prisonwall.org

Victim Assistance Online: A Comprehensive Resource Center
www.vaonline.org

## Organizations

Angel Tree: A Ministry for Prison Fellowship (camping or Christmas gifts for prisoner's children)
P. O. Box 1550
Merrifield, VA 22116–1550
800–55–ANGEL
www.christianity.com/angeltree

Family and Corrections Network (a listing of all related government agencies and assistance organizations)
The Incarcerated Fathers Library
32 Oak Grove Rd.
Palmyra, VA 22963
434–589–3036
www.fcnetwork.org

National Youth Court Center (for information about teen courts)
c/o American Probation and Parole Association
P. O. Box 11910
Lexington, KY
40578–1910

859–244–8215
www.youthcourt.net

United States Parole Commission
5550 Friendship Blvd., Suite 420
Chevy Chase, MD 20815–7286
301–492–5990
www.usdoj.gov/prisoninfo.htm

Volunteers of America (runs several programs to assist with
transition/reintegration as well as hospice/palliative care for terminally ill inmates)
1660 Duke St.
Alexandria, VA 22314–3427
800–899–0089
www.voa.org

Young Audiences of North Texas Creative Solutions (conducts "in
facility" art programs for youth)
4145 Travis St., Suite 201
Dallas, TX 01901
214–520–9988
www.yanorthtexas.org/community/at_risk_teens.htm

# DISABILITIES AND ABILITIES

*Our chief want in life is somebody who shall make us do what we can.*
—Ralph Waldo Emerson

The best advice anyone can give a volunteer interested in helping people with disabilities—ranging from mobility impairment and chronic illnesses to auditory impairments and traumatic brain injuries—is to focus on what the individual *can* do. How can you help them achieve maximum independence, participate in rewarding endeavors, and ultimately assist others?

● Groups
♥ Families
★ Youth
♥ Professional Qualifications
ℛ Training Required

*Always refer to a "person," not a "disabled person."*

*Talk to people with blindness or visual impairments in a normal voice; they can probably hear fine.*

*Acknowledge people in wheelchairs. Meet them at their eye level first, then focus on others at your level that may be escorting them.*

*Look directly at people who are deaf or hearing impaired. They probably read lips well.*

*Take advantage of screening programs for children three through six years of age to identify amblyopia (lazy eye) and other critical vision problems.*

*Take precautions against injuries and falling; wear a seatbelt.*

*Be patient with victims of severe brain injuries. They typically face five to ten years of intensive rehabilitation.*

*Don't even think about using handicapped parking if you aren't disabled. Think about how much harder it would be for people with disabilities to gain access where you're going.*

*Be supportive of people with learning disabilities. They will "catch up" with age and experience and can advance in almost any profession.*

## INDEPENDENT LIVING

Almost two-thirds of people with disabilities are unemployed, while others manage their households, have full-time jobs, drive their own cars, and are buying homes. Doing the basic activities of daily living takes more time and energy for a person with disabilities. A little extra help may allow people who are disabled to complete advanced schooling, keep a job, and stay in their homes. Volunteers can provide significant service by assisting with:

- Grocery shopping ♥ ★
- Picking up prescriptions ♥ ★
- Running household errands ♥ ★
- Housekeeping ● ♥ ★
- Performing home repairs ● ♥ ★
- Gardening ● ♥ ★

*Anyone who can use a drill and a saw can put together a ramp.*

*—Melissa Hoffman, Accessibility Design Coordinator*

Architectural firms, contractors, business organizations, and governmental agencies can fill important roles that will improve life in the community for people with disabilities, but service groups and handy individuals can do as much to help in neighborhoods and homes:

- Solve site accessibility problems in the community. ♥

- Assess and design home modifications for people with disabilities. ♥

- Build wheelchair ramps according to legal and physical specifications. ● ♥ ★ ໃ

- Widen existing doors and install grab bars or transfer seats in a bathroom. ● ♥ ♥ ໃ

Centers for independent living provide services to help people with disabilities learn to live on their own. Many staff members at such centers are people with disabilities who teach from personal experience. Centers are always looking for volunteers who are active and able to assist in training activities.

People who are hospitalized for severe illnesses and who don't have family members close by may find themselves released to nursing homes. They may also need training on site to help them adjust to a new lifestyle. Volunteers are needed at independent living centers to:

- Assist people with learning basic living skills. ໃ

- Train people in financial management. ♥  ໃ

- Teach pre-vocational skills. ໃ

- Assist in teaching personal attendant/management skills. ໃ

- Provide one-on-one skill training for people in nursing homes. ໃ

## RECREATIONAL PROGRAMS

Organizations that focus on recreational opportunities for people with disabilities are generally prepared to accommodate any impairment—orthopedic, spinal cord, neuromuscular, visual, hearing, cognitive, and developmental. Their mission is to empower individuals to reach their full potential, which may ultimately include rock climbing, canoeing, cycling, horseback riding, golf—you name it. With adaptive equipment and a group of well-trained volunteers, almost anything is possible. Recreational groups emphasize safety, education, and fun and attract medical and business professionals, education and recreation specialists, as well as fun-loving adults, students, and youth as volunteers. Here are some of the things volunteers might be asked to do:

- Assist with outdoor recreation outings. ★ ⚹

- Become a peer leader of youth with disabilities. ★ ⚹

- Teach adapted basketball, track, T-ball, aquatics, and soccer. ★ ⚹

- Coach/assist with Special Olympics, Paralympics, and other events. ★ ⚹

---

*I can watch or I can say, "I have that inside of me, I can do it. I can go for it."*

*I used to get condescending remarks all the time, but I grew up feeling equal with my sisters and brother.*

*It's that fighting sense in me that wants to exceed others' expectations. I want to feel like I can do anything. . . . Since I got that first Paralympic gold medal in slalom I no longer get just a pat on the back. Now people say, "You are good."*

—Lacey Heward, won two bronze medals in the 2002 Winter Paralympic Games

---

## VISUAL AND HEARING DISABILITIES

There are a host of special programs and tools that assist those with visual and audio impairments. Here are some ways you can help:

- Encourage people who are newly disabled to attend training and adjustment classes in orientation and mobility, Braille, computer training, activities of daily living, diabetic management, and crafts. Be aware that there are vocational rehabilitation services and business enterprise programs that assist in retraining a person to operate and manage a private business. ● ♥ ★

- Help people with low or failing vision get to low vision clinics for optical and non-optical aids (i.e., magnifying lenses, talking clocks, and scales, large-number phones, Braille watches, digital talking books, and so on). ♥

- Escort people with visual impairments on shopping trips. Let them hold on to you rather than you holding on to them. Ask them questions, "What are you interested in?" Describe the whole picture. "This is the aisle with tools, glassware, toys . . ." Don't leave them; if you're going to walk away, always say where you're going. Help them touch something they are interested in so they are not fishing in the air. ♥ ★

- Learn to finger spell.

- Take people with visual impairments to places of interest—study groups for the blind, classes for the blind (in knitting, ceramics, refinishing furniture, and so on), church services, and concerts. ● ♥ ★

- Read the news aloud to individuals at blind centers or in their homes (or try contacting radio stations that sponsor newspaper coverage). ● ♥ ★

Volunteering is never limited to those without any disabilities. Here are a few ways that people with hearing impairments can help:

- Adults can mentor younger people.

- Younger people can mentor seniors with late-onset hearing disabilities. ★

- Hard of hearing people can serve in the community by helping people learn to read, use computers, understand the Internet, build houses (Habitat for Humanity), and care for children with severe disabilities. ● ♥ ★

---

*What I love is a sense of humor. I have diabetes in my family and I look to the people in the ceramics class for the blind as my heroes; I may be in their situation some day. For instance, Jim wants his epitaph to read, "See you later." Ann passed me scissors the other day saying, "Can't you see these aren't worth beans?" And when our instructor wasn't here Marie said, "We're like the blind leading the blind."*

*—Betty Hendren, volunteer*

## Brain Injuries

Brain injuries occur more frequently than breast cancer, AIDS, Multiple Sclerosis, and spinal cord injury. Allan I. Bergman, president and CEO of the Brain Injury Association, says brain injuries are a "silent epidemic" that is the leading cause of death and disability in children and young adults (in "Harris Poll Shows Low Public Awareness of Brain Injury," *Making Headway*, no. 3, 2001, 5). For those who survive, brain injuries are life altering, causing serious physical impairments and a variety of cognitive, behavioral, and emotional complications. The Traumatic Brain Injury Act of 1996 is making available resources for computer-intensive one-on-one exercises for adults. Everyone can make a difference to those who experience such injuries by:

> *We all have disabilities; we all have areas of strength; we all have areas of weakness. Employers are happy to work with our people if they are trained.*
>
> —*Paul Barnes, employment specialist, Brain Injury Association*

*Accepting the change; don't compare people to their past*

*Encouraging retraining; focus on what people can learn to do now*

*Hiring individuals with brain injuries at meaningful jobs during the gradual stages of regeneration*

## More Ideas for Expanding Service

There is no end to the ways individuals and organizations can help people with disabilities. Many marvelous ideas are in motion that can in turn spawn others. The nicest thing about helping is that the rewards are immediate; creative programs empower people with disabilities. Here is just a sampling of the possibilities:

- Theaters can provide audio description performances for the blind and signing for the deaf.

- Companies can train people with disabilities to conduct access surveys, which help evaluate what facilities are accessible to people with disabilities.

- Dance centers can involve dancers with disabilities; choreographers may create and produce numbers for wheelchair dance companies.

- Art centers may sponsor art classes and museum exhibits that enable people with disabilities to develop and share their talents.

- Business institutes can teach micro business and small business training programs to people with disabilities.

- Women's organizations in the United States can help women in third-world countries improve the lives of people with disabilities (for example, teach women how to create wheelchairs out of materials they can find locally).

- Film festivals can be sponsored by, for, and about people with disabilities.

- Career men and women with disabilities can mentor people with disabilities who are just getting started in a career.

- School districts may sponsor invitational games for students too severely disabled to participate in the Special Olympics.

*One boy walked around with his high school peer buddy—didn't want to play many games, just walk around and hang out. It was such fun to see him enjoy being a teenager, not a "disabled kid." When working with these more severely impaired students, I'm convinced the joy is as much for the families, who sometimes feel their children are cheated, as it is for the students themselves.*

*—Midge Evans, special education teacher*

## To Volunteer

Contact any of the following groups:

Alternatives programs
Centers for disabilities services in universities

Community Centers
Independent living centers
Paralympics
Special Olympics
State brain injury associations
State divisions of services for the blind and visually impaired
State divisions of services for the deaf and hard of hearing
Transitional living centers

## Suggested Reading

*The Assist Guidebook to the Accessible Home: Practical Designs for Home Modifications.* Available for $10.00 from Assist, Inc., 218 East 500 South, Salt Lake City, UT 84111. 801–355–7085

*Putting Creativity to Work: Careers in the Arts for People with Disabilities* (a free publication from the Social Security Administration). Fax request to 410–965–2037. www.vsarts.org/resources/publications/careerguide

## Internet Resources

ADA: Americans with Disabilities Act Information Resources
www.adata.org

Disabled Sports USA
www.dsusa.org

Ethel Louise Armstrong Foundation (complete list of disability portals)
www.ela.org

Library Resources for the Blind and Physically Handicapped
www.loc.gov/nls

VSA Arts (educational and career resources for people with disabilities)
www.vsarts.org

## Organizations

AGBell: Alexander Graham Bell Association for the Deaf and Hard of Hearing
4317 Volta Pl., NW
Washington D.C. 20007
202–337–5330 (voice)
202–337–5221 (TTY)
www.agbell.org

Brain Injury Association
105 N. Alfred St.
Alexandria, VA 22314
800–444–6443 (family helpline)
www.biausa.org

Easter Seals (for help with events and camps for people with disabilities)
230 West Monroe St., Suite 1800
Chicago, IL 60606
800–221–6827
www.easter-seals.org

National Ability Center (a recreational center and ranch)
P. O. Box 682799
Quinn's Junction, Highways 248 & 40
Park City, UT 84068
435–649–3991
www.nationalabilitycenter.org

SHHH: Self Help for Hard of Hearing People
7910 Woodmont Ave., Suite 1200
Bethesda, MD 20814
301–657–2248
www.shhh.org

## Other Resources

Adaptive Environments (offers a publication on home adaptation for persons with disabilities with lists of products and assistance resources)
374 Congress St., Suite 301
Boston, MA 02210
617–695–1225
www.adaptiveenvironments.org

National Library Service for the Blind and Physically Handicapped
Library of Congress
Washington D.C. 20542
202–707–5100
www.loc.gov/nls

# EDUCATION

*A mind once stretched by a new idea never regains its original dimension.*
—*Oliver Wendell Holmes*

No longer are the "Three Rs" reading, writing, and arithmetic. The Three Rs are now Relationships, Resilience, and Readiness (see Richard W. Riley, "What Students Need to Succeed," The National Association of Partners in Education

- ● Groups
- ♥ Families
- ★ Youth
- ♛ Professional Qualifications
- ☉ Training Required

and Search Institute [Brochure], n.d.). Society has learned that it is no longer enough for young people to stay in school and avoid drugs; they need the kind of integral education that will prepare them to become productive workers, loving parents, and contributing citizens. At the same time, the adult workplace also requires increasing proficiency in math, science, reading, and technology skills. American manufacturers say that at least half of all job applicants are rejected as unqualified and that high school job training programs are inadequate (See *Needed: A Prepared Workforce*, National Association of Manufacturers, 2000). Everyone can help with this growing problem and thus make a difference to a child or teenager's education by doing the following:

> *Read, listen, and discuss with children their hobbies, travels, and school activities.*
>
> *Ask and answer questions of youth—about careers, colleges, social problems, and current events.*

*Supply details on local history; describe your participation in historic events.*

*Invite student groups to see your work place, your volunteer post, your hobby room, your music studio, and so on.*

## ELEMENTARY SCHOOLS

School volunteers have become critical members of education teams in local communities. Volunteers should be individuals who *like* children, want to *help* the school, and have *time* to devote a few hours a week to the task. The greatest benefit for school volunteers is that teaching is learning—about new skills, about children, and about the community.

The opportunities for helping children (ages five through eleven) at elementary schools are many:

> *Talking to those first graders made it as memorable a Veteran's Day as riding in a tank for the parade forty years ago. I was hesitant, but the teacher had the children make up questions. They wanted to know if I flew a helicopter, if I was frightened, what I ate, and how I felt when my buddies got hurt—a whole slew of things. By the time it was over I had really enjoyed myself, and I think they learned a thing or two.*
>
> *—Ray Alto, senior volunteer*

- Listen to children read; tell stories.
- Reinforce learning of the alphabet or recognition of numbers as a classroom aide.
- Conduct flash card and color word drills.
- Set up or assist in learning centers.
- Assist in school clinics or libraries.
- Compile a list of library resources available at the school.
- Help office workers contact parents.
- Visit a sick child: deliver materials and bring completed homework back to the school (requires a background check).

- Practice vocabulary with foreign students; help children learn a foreign language.
- Make or play instructional games.
- Play games at recess; help young children to walk on a balance beam, jump rope, or skip.
- Prepare bulletin boards and other visual materials for classrooms and hallways.
- Supervise groups taking a test; grade papers.
- Work with underachievers or children with disabilities.
- Help select or donate books for the school library.
- Gather resource materials.
- Help set up experiments in science classrooms or other applicable areas.
- Help with cooking projects; teach children to sew, knit.
- Play a musical instrument; help students who play instruments.
- Make puppets for a classroom; dramatize a story.
- Help with handwriting practice.
- Drill spelling words.
- Set up a "grocery store" to practice math skills.

In some neighborhoods, a whole battery of volunteers is needed to help before and after school hours with some of the following tasks:

- Act as safety guards before and after school. ● ♥ ★
- Monitor the schoolyard to keep it safe for play into the evenings and on weekends. ● ♥ ★
- Coach after-school teams. ★
- Act as homework tutors after hours. ● ★
- Volunteer as field trip leaders. ● ★

- Offer pro bono medical and dental care at the school after hours. ♥

## SECONDARY SCHOOLS

If you are more interested in helping in secondary education schools, you might want to try volunteering in one of the following ways:

- Give language students extra practice in conversation (requires training in specific language). ★

- Answer questions about careers, training opportunities, and college selection.

- Contribute to social studies units: discuss urban renewal and social programs.

- Help students use library sources and assist with research projects.

- Teach cardiopulmonary resuscitation to health classes. ● ♥

- Tape record textbooks for students with reading disabilities. ★

- Prepare materials for visually impaired students with computers or Brailling machines. ★ ⚡

- Assist in science, math, computer, and vocational laboratories. ⚡

- Arrange meaningful field trips into the community.

- Sponsor school clubs and interest groups.

- Assist with the production of videocassettes and other audio-visual products. ●

- Help students with school publications and productions.

- Produce a parent-teacher newsletter.

- Assist English teachers as lay readers of student essays and compositions.

- Help students who were absent to make up missed work. ★

If you do choose to volunteer at an elementary or secondary school, be aware that volunteers in schools must follow five specific guidelines to assure effective participation:

1. Assist only as requested.

2. Commit to a schedule.

3. Maintain confidentiality.

4. Use appropriate channels of communication.

5. Integrate into the present school program.

> There was a tough group of sixth graders one year. They had been stigmatized as low achievers with behavioral problems, not really into sports. But, Shakespeare—the whole idea of a play was so difficult no one could deny success would be truly great. I cut the play to an hour, but that was still 300 lines of Macbeth! Every child had a part (we double cast), every line was memorized, and by the time we finished four weeks of rehearsals, every child knew everyone's part—they quoted lines back and forth in the hall. Other parents helped by coaching individual scenes, some designed scenery. Fitting costumes, putting on makeup, people were paying attention to these kids individually. And during the performance the students made their discovery— not only was the story significant but they were phenomenal, better than anyone had ever thought.
>
> —Karen Maxwell, parent volunteer

## PARTNERS IN EDUCATION

Throughout the United States, local businesses and even large companies have begun forming partnerships with schools in an effort to boost community pride, values, and growth. Goals are usually specific to the locality. But the aim of all such partnerships is to prepare students for meaningful employment, lifelong learning, and community service. Businesses may volunteer by:

- Providing guest speakers in classrooms. ♥

- Providing schools with Junior Achievement volunteers (business community volunteers trained to inspire young people in the value of free enterprise). ❤

- Providing job-mentoring opportunities for students.

- Providing internships, apprenticeships, or cooperative education opportunities for students and teachers.

- Assisting teachers in classroom settings.

- Hosting classroom field trips.

- Participating in career fairs.

- Providing training on computer literacy and real world applications to teachers and parents (for example, a company may mentor the at-risk population of their community by sponsoring weekly breakfasts and plant tours).

- Donating materials (hospitals, for example, may offer equipment needed to complete a science lab).

One unique business-education partnership is Groundhog Job Shadow Day. This is a national opportunity for educators and employers to help youth develop motivation and make decisions about their future. Teachers identify interested students, who then make plans to shadow an employee of a local business. A student interested in a career in journalism, for example, may visit a newsroom for the day. Employers work through the Junior Achievement program and encourage employees to become mentors. Employees spend the day helping their assigned students understand the skills and academics needed in their career field.

## NATIONAL SERVICE-LEARNING PROGRAM

At college and university levels, community-education partnerships are working to provide character education through service–learning opportunities. "Service-learning is a form of experiential education where learning occurs through a cycle of action and reflection as students work with others through a process of applying what they are learning to community problems and, at the same time, reflecting upon their experience as they seek to achieve real objectives for the community and deeper understanding and skills for themselves" (Janet Eyler and Dwight E. Giles, *Where's the Learning in Service-Learning?* San Francisco: Jossey-Bass, 1999).

> We had an architectural student do her service-learning requirement with us for a semester. She went in the outreach van to help check on the homeless— along the waterways and by the railroad tracks. During her first reflection session she said, "They're gross, they stink." . . . In the last session of the semester she said, "I've been spoiled. I've had everything provided my whole life. Categorizing the homeless is wrong. We have to help them one by one."
>
> —Janeal Ford, volunteer coordinator, Volunteers of America

Among other things, service-learning programs provide universities with the option of offering enriched diplomas to students who have received training in community service and who practice regular volunteerism. Service-learning programs provide intellectual, civic, ethical, cross-cultural, career, and other personal training to students of all ages.

In the past decade, college students in record numbers have felt compelled to confront society's problems by helping through service-learning programs. And similar programs are now expanding quickly into the nation's secondary schools (and more recently into the primary grades).

If you're interested in participating in a service-learning program, visit the National Service-Learning Clearinghouse at http://www.servicelearning.org.

## ALUMNI

Checking out the needs of an alma mater is a customized way to perpetuate education. And reconnecting with your past to help others achieve their potential can be immensely satisfying. Some alums return to provide service to their elementary and secondary schools, others to their former colleges and universities. Alumni volunteers can help their alma maters by:

- Tutoring

- Supporting the sports program and booster clubs ●
- Starting an after-school club ●
- Helping students with college financial aid applications and SAT preparation
- Taking notes, reading texts, or scribing during exams for students with disabilities

## LITERACY

A study by the United States Department of Education, which measured the literacy skills of a random sample of more than 26,000 individuals in the United States aged sixteen years and older, found that more than 20 percent of American adults are functioning at the lowest level. At most, these individuals can total the entry on a bank deposit slip or locate information in a short news article. But many do so with difficulty, and others can't at all ("STATS: National Adult Literacy Survey," Syracuse, N.Y.: Laubach Literacy Action Information Center, 1993).

> *One of the best ways to show children you care is to take the time to read with them. Reading is the foundation of learning and the golden door to opportunity. For students who don't learn to read well in the early years of elementary school, it is virtually impossible to keep up in the later years. That's why literacy programs are so important. They give young children realistic opportunities to learn to read and to practice their reading.*
>
> *—Senator Edward M. Kennedy, volunteer reading mentor*

Tutoring adults in literacy is one of the best ways to serve another individual. Help from volunteer tutors is needed by a wide variety of community agencies that serve many individuals.

Through training, tutors can quickly acquire the following skills needed for success in the literacy program:

- Identifying the special characteristics and needs of adult learners (lack of self-esteem, health, or family issues).

- Assessing instructional approaches (choosing a theme-based, phonics-based, or integrated reading, writing, and reasoning approach designed for pre-GED level).

• Adapting to the needs and interests of an individual (a native English or foreign-language speaker, a prisoner, or a mentally impaired individual, for example).

• Using visual materials (newspapers, library books, maps, props) to teach skills.

## LIBRARIES

Education is unlimited and free to those who use public libraries. Many facilities, however, are under-funded and in great need of volunteer help to do some of the following tasks:

• Work at the information desk, giving directions and helping users locate books. ★ ⚥

• Serve as Internet docents by assisting users in finding Internet sites and using the library's search program. ★ ⚥

• Repair books, clean books, and rewind tapes. ★ ⚥

• Shelve books. ★ ⚥

• Shelf read (which entails adopting a favorite section and keeping it in order). ★ ⚥

• Deliver books to seniors and the housebound. "Operation Homebound" may include matching appropriate books with the homebound person and getting to know that person. ♥ ★ ⚥

• Create artistic displays. ★

• Provide clerical help. ★ ⚥

• Assist with children's story hour, including preparing materials. ★ ⚥

• Join the Friends of the Library association (members help with book sales and special events). ● ♥ ★

## Suggested Reading

Barbara Rogoff, Carolyn Goodman Turkanis, Leslee Bartlett, eds.,
*Learning Together: Children and Adults in a School Community*, New
York: Oxford University Press, 2001.

## Internet Resources:

Adult Literacy Estimates
http://casas.org/lit/litcode/search.cfm

Elementary Educators (sampling of visual aids and lesson resources available online)
http://k-6educators.about.com

Literacy Volunteers of America, Inc.
www.literacyvolunteers.org

National Institute for Literacy
www.nifl.gov

National Service-Learning Clearinghouse
866–245–7378
www.servicelearning.org

Secondary School Educators (sampling of visual aids and lesson
resources available online)
http://7-12educators.about.com

Science and Math Initiatives (comprehensive list of classroom resources
for science and math)
www.learner.org

## Organizations

Adult Education and Literacy Division (largest adult basic skills program
in U.S.)
Office of Vocational and Adult Education
Department of Education
400 Maryland Ave., SW
Washington D.C. 20202–0498
800–USA–LEARN (800–872–5327)
www.ed.gov/offices/OVAE/AdultEd/

America's Promise—The Alliance for Youth (community partnering, individual tutoring)
909 North Washington St., Suite 400
Alexandria, VA 22314–1556
888–55–YOUTH
www.americaspromise.org

"I Have a Dream" Foundation, The (long-term educational support program for children from low-income communities)
330 Seventh Ave., 20th Floor
New York, NY 10001
212–293–5480
www.ihad.org

Junior Achievement, Inc. (educating youth in the value of free enterprise)
National Headquarters
One Education Way
Colorado Springs, CO 80906–4477
719–540–8000
www.ja.org

Laubach Literacy Action (materials on how to start a volunteer literacy program)
Attention: Program Management Coordinator
1320 Jamesville Ave., Box 131
Syracuse, NY 13210
315–422–9121
www.laubach.org

National Association of Partners in Education (partnerships to improve academic and personal growth of youth)
901 N. Pitt St., Suite 320
Alexandria, VA 22314
703–836–4880
www.napehq.org

National Groundhog Job Shadow Day Coalition
1901 L. St. NW, Suite 300
Washington D.C. 20036
800–373–3174
www.jobshadow.org

National PTA (parent and public involvement to support children and
   youth in education)
330 N. Wabash Ave., Suite 2100
Chicago, IL 60611
800–307–4PTA
www.pta.org

Search Institute (resources on building community assets to strengthen
   youth)
The Banks Building
615 First Ave., NE, Suite 125
Minneapolis, MN 55413
612–379–4930
www.searchinstitute.org

# ENVIRONMENT: PARKS AND GARDENS

*Come forth into the light of things. Let Nature be your teacher.*
—*William Wordsworth*

To value nature is to perpetuate beauty, to reverence God, and to serve our fellow beings. Natural beauty deserves awareness and care. As the population expands, each of us gains more responsibility. Following the rules is essential.

| | |
|---|---|
| ● | Groups |
| ♥ | Families |
| ★ | Youth |
| ♥ | Professional Qualifications |
| ⚡ | Training Required |

Parents, youth leaders, and all other adults must be accountable for teaching the next generation to respect and preserve the environment. Here are a few things everyone can do to make a difference:

*Pack it in—pack it out.*

*Stay on the straight and narrow (no trail breaking).*

*Leave no mark.*

*Recycle.*

*Conserve water and other natural resources.*

## HABITAT

Conserving nature sustains life. But replenishing nature *renews* the earth and its people. Planting is an act of personal stewardship that will benefit the world today and bless the generations of tomorrow. Here are some ideas for serving and *preserving* our habitat:

- Plant a tree. The last Friday in April is National Arbor Day, but other states have chosen dates to accommodate their climate (January in Florida and November in Hawaii, for example). ● ♥ ★

- Create a natural wildlife habitat in your backyard. To do so, plant native varieties of vegetation. Essential elements include food (such as plants that produce acorns, nuts, berries, seeds, buds, nectar, and pollen), water (like a bird bath or small pond), cover (a variety of plants ranging in size and density, including both evergreen and deciduous species). ♥ ★

- Create a schoolyard habitat, work place habitat, or community wildlife habitat. ● ★

- Become a "Habitat Steward" (a mentor who helps others create or restore natural habitats). ⚡

Individual states and cities may sponsor "take pride" days or join in the annual Great American Cleanup day, in which local groups find a project, coordinate one assigned by the state, or simply register individually to assist as volunteers (for state listings, visit www.kab.org). Projects might include:

> *No shade tree? Blame not the sun but yourself.*
>
> *—Chinese Proverb*

- Building and maintaining trails. ● ♥ ★

- Cleaning up neighborhoods and roadways (Adopt a Highway is one particular program). ● ♥ ★

- Removing material from "unsanctioned" dumping sites. ● ♥ ★

- Volunteering to do archaeological work on public lands. ●

- Ridding rangelands and farmlands of noxious weeds. ● ★

- Doing restoration work at state and federal camp-grounds. ●
- Preserving a natural park in an urban area. ● ♥ ★
- Removing graffiti from public areas. ● ♥ ★

## PARKS

Parks and recreation centers, as well as historic preservation sites, use volunteers on a regular basis. Most programs are locally administered. One might volunteer to:

- Assist with a flower and garden show, an Easter egg hunt, or a harvest festival at the community recreation center. ● ♥ ★
- Beautify city or county parks by doing weeding and edging (contact your city or county parks and recreation division; youth groups need a supervisor). ● ♥ ★
- Virtually adopt a neighborhood park, planning special events and clean-up days. ● ♥ ★
- Volunteer at historic park sites as tour guides and interpreters of local history. (Some dress in costumes to depict the mood of the times they describe.) ♥ ★

State parks look for volunteers to:

- Host a campground for a season. (Hosts provide their own motor home or trailer and are given a free camp-site in exchange for posting reservations, performing light maintenance on restrooms, and providing information and assistance to visitors.) ♥ ⚲
- Staff information booths. ⚲
- Conduct interpretive programs. ⚲
- Monitor wildlife. ⚲
- Garden/landscape. ● ♥ ★
- Paint/repair/restore buildings. ● ♥ ★
- Clear trails. ● ♥ ★

- Clean up parks and streams. ● ♥ ★

There are more volunteer opportunities than there are paying jobs at national parks. Each of the 376 units of the National Park Service has a Volunteers in Parks Program (VIP), which is administered locally but listed on the Internet (http://www.nps. gov/volunteer/) or is available by phone (202–208–4747). Though volunteers are not paid, some parks do reimburse volunteers for out-of-pocket expenses, such as local travel costs, meals, and uniforms. Other National Park Service opportunities include:

- Archaeology and ethnography fieldwork ⚥
- Museum management programs ⚥
- National trails maintenance ●

---

**Why Plant Trees?**

- Tree leaves clean the air; one tree can absorb 26 pounds of carbon dioxide.
- Planting trees results in improved water quality by slowing rainfall runoff and preventing soil erosion.
- Trees around buildings can reduce air conditioning needs by 30 percent and heating costs by 20 to 50 percent.
- Trees provide shelter for wildlife, muffle noise, and provide privacy.
- Trees can instill community pride; police officers believe that trees and landscaping help cool tempers in hot summer months.
- Trees add to property values.
- In laboratory research, visual exposure to settings with trees has produced significant recovery from stress within five minutes, as indicated by changes in blood pressure and muscle tension.

—Dr. Roger S. Ulrich, Texas A&M University

---

## GARDENING TO SHARE

Gardens can bring security, give variety, and build values in individuals, families, and other groups. Many people like to grow fruits, vegetables, herbs, and flowers to save money, to guarantee freshness, or to enjoy relaxed exercise out-of-doors. Gardens may now have enlarged purpose and scope. Food banks are frequently

> *What the earth really needs is a good housekeeper.*
>
> *—Aviva Rahmani, artist/ecological rehabilitator*

without fresh produce, while gardeners often raise more than they can use or have time to harvest. With a garden, you can help your local food bank by:

- Planting a "Row for the Hungry" in your own garden. Plant vegetables and fruits that travel well and are good keepers: broccoli, cabbage, carrots, peas, green beans, tomatoes, sweet peppers, eggplants, squash, onions, beets, apples, pears—even herbs are welcome. (Discuss other ideas with the group to which you'll be contributing—climate dictates what's easy to grow and most enjoyed by locals.) ● ♥ ★

- Harvesting and thoroughly cleaning produce. If you maintain a large, commercial garden, ask school groups, youth groups, or church groups for help at this stage. ● ♥ ★

- Delivering produce to designated drop-offs. Contact your local food bank, soup kitchen, church, social agency, or Salvation Army for information. ● ♥ ★

- Gathering the produce from drop-off sites and delivering it to distribution centers. ● ♥ ★

## GARDENING IN THE COMMUNITY

The typical home garden—especially with vegetables—is no longer attainable for most city dwellers. Community gardens have sprung up all over America during the last two decades to compensate. What can you do at the community garden?

- First, join one. Community gardens give beauty and vitality to cities, they:

  Unite a neighborhood/community

  Foster intergenerational relationships (plants that fascinate all ages include popcorn, sunflower seeds, loofah sponges, decorative gourds, small pumpkins)

Provide education (gardeners may meet together for a lecture about herbs)

Offer recreation (gardening is good exercise and may be enhanced when groups gather at the garden for morning yoga)

Provide relaxation (benches may be added where people read, sun, and chat)

Allow refugees and immigrants to plant their traditional foods, which may not be available in supermarkets

- Volunteer in the youth plots of community gardens. ●
  ⚔

- Help high-school students gain employment through "Youth-at-Market" programs, where students donate produce they grow during the week to the food bank and sell the rest at the Farmer's Market on the weekend.

- Work alongside inner-city and at-risk kids in youth development programs. You'll be teaching them how to garden but they may learn respect, responsibility, and cooperation as well.

- Become a Master Gardener (Programs in all states offer a minimum of fifty hours of instruction plus fifty hours of volunteer service, such as answering gardening questions by phone, conducting workshops, working with 4–H youth, and donating home-grown produce to the needy. Retaining your status as a Master Gardener requires ongoing volunteer service hours and annual advanced training). ⚔

## GARDEN/BOTANICAL VOLUNTEERS

Helping at botanical gardens, arboretums, and conservatories is both educational and rewarding. Volunteers are needed to:

- Teach school groups in a natural setting. ⚔

- Train as a naturalist/horticulturist and become a garden guide or a station host. ✗

- Work side-by-side with professional gardeners in the greenhouse or on the grounds. ★ ✗

- Assist with labeling and watering plants. ★ ✗

Dan Underwood, a former public housing resident, has worked with more than 150 children directing this after-school project, dubbed Cabrini-Greens. The kids work five days a week growing "designer" organic lettuce like mesclun mix escarole. They then sell the produce to some of Chicago's fanciest restaurants and natural supermarkets and split the profits. Each child earns up to $700 per planting season, depending on their age and how many hours they work. It's a rare patch of hope in one of the most hopeless areas of the country.

—Warren Cohen

## More Ideas for Expanding Service

Looking for more outdoor service ideas? Try one of the following:

- Create sculptures to house filtering systems for water purification. Beach trash may be turned into wonderful driftwood, metal, and plastic sculptures. ● ♥ ★

- Start up gardens for specific groups in need of a project, such as former inmates who can work for an hourly wage or people in wheelchairs who can work with raised planter boxes. ● ♥ ★

- Turn environmental liabilities into spots of beauty. Landscape around a junk car in the backyard or junkyards on a highway. ● ♥ ★

- Offer free landscaping courses in particularly blighted areas to neighborhood residents. ♥

## Suggested Reading

Karen Payne and Deborah Fryman, *Cultivating Community: Principles and Practices for Community Gardening As a Community-Building Tool.* (Order from The American Community Gardening Association for $10.)

## Internet Resources

Cultural Resources Diversity Initiative of the National Park Service (lists volunteer positions in archaeology, historic places, and museums)
www.cr.nps.gov/getinvol.htm

My Master Gardener Page (description of Master Gardener program and state listings)
www.hal-pc.org/~trobb/mastgar.html

Plant a Row for the Hungry
www.gwaa.org/par/index.html
877–GWAA–PAR

Student Conservation Association (hands-on outdoor volunteer work for youth)
www.sca-inc.org

U.S./Canadian Parks
www.usparks.about.com

## Organizations

American Community Gardening Association
100 N. 20th St., 5th Floor
Philadelphia, PA 19103–1495
215–988–8800
www.communitygarden.org

Keep America Beautiful (information on 500 local affiliates that support cleanup days)
1010 Washington Blvd.
Stafford, CT 06901
203–323–8987
www.kab.org

National Arbor Day Foundation
211 N. 12th St.
Lincoln, NE 68508
402–474–5655
www.arborday.org

National Park Service: Volunteers-in-Parks
P. O. Box 37127
Washington D.C. 20013–7127
202–208–4747
www.nps.gov/volunteer

National Wildlife Federation (information on creating wildlife habitats)
11100 Wildlife Center Drive
Reston, VA 20190–5362
800–822–9919
http://www.nwf.org/backyardwildlifehabitat/

Other outdoor volunteer work is available through:

Bureau of Land Management (www.blm.gov/nhp)
Christian Ministry in National Parks (www.coolworks.com/natprk.htm)
National Audubon Society (www.audubon.org)
Sierra Club (www.sierraclub.org)

# FIRE AND
# EMERGENCY SERVICES

*It is by presence of mind in untried emergencies that the native mettle of a man is tested.*

—*Abraham Lincoln*

In emergency situations, volunteering is often spontaneous. People who happen to be on the scene at the time help out as they can. For this reason, it's important that everyone have some training in emergency response. It's also important that families and individuals have their homes prepared for

● **Groups**
♥ **Families**
★ **Youth**
♥ **Professional Qualifications**
Ɣ **Training Required**

emergency situations. Everyone can make a difference in this area by doing the following things:

*Coordinate family communications in case of an emergency.*

*Designate places for family members to meet outside the home (for fire), and outside the neighborhood (if you can't get home).*

*Pick a "family contact" out-of-state (for a widespread emergency to whom all family members can phone in with their locations).*

*Learn how to turn off the water, gas, and electricity at your residence.*

*Install at least one smoke detector on every floor (replace batteries every year); buy fire extinguishers (date and replace every 6 years).*

*Keep an emergency kit on hand in an easy-to-carry container, such as a backpack, suitcase, or covered trash container. Stock it with the following items:*

*a supply of food and water for three days for each member of the family*

*a change of clothing, blanket, and sleeping bag for each family member*

*a first-aid kit and medications*

*a battery operated radio and flashlight with extra batteries*

*extra car keys, cash, credit card*

*important documents in a waterproof container*

*sanitation supplies*

*Know your neighbors: What are their special skills? What are their individual needs? Are there children or elderly people living in your neighborhood? Do they have disabilities?*

## FIRE

Fires kill more Americans than all natural disasters combined (including floods, hurricanes, tornadoes, earthquakes, and other natural disasters). Eighty percent of fire fatalities occur in residences, with cooking as the leading cause. Although 88 percent of homes have at least one smoke alarm, there has been a disturbing increase over the last decade of fires in homes with non-functioning alarms. Everyone can make a difference and help prevent or avoid injury from fires by doing the following:

*The fire department doesn't inspect houses unless specifically requested by the occupants, but anyone can pick up an inspection form like we use for buildings, and it might help.*

*Some people die because they can't get out of their homes in an emergency. If you have a dead bolt lock on a door or on window bars, you've got to keep the key in it. If you have a wood-burning fireplace you have to know what you're going to do with live ashes. And people with garages attached to the house should have carbon monoxide detectors—they make great Christmas gifts.*

*—Marty Peterson, Captain, Salt Lake City Fire Department*

*Practice escape plans as if there were a fire:*

*Plan two ways of escape from every room—to a safe meeting place outside.*

*Practice alerting household members—keep a bell and flashlight in each room.*

*Practice evacuating blindfolded—the amount of smoke generated by a fire will likely make it impossible to see.*

*Practice staying low to the ground and covering mouth with a cloth or clothing while escaping.*

*Feel all doors before opening them; if the door is hot, get out another way. Close doors in each room after escaping.*

*Learn to stop, drop to the ground, and roll if clothes catch fire.*

*If you build your home near wildland vegetation, maintain it using all the safety precautions:*

*Build with fire-resistant materials (tile or metal siding for roofs, thick tempered safety glass in windows).*

*Create a safety zone to separate the home from combustible plants and vegetation.*

*Learn and teach outdoor fire safety:*

*Build fires away from nearby trees or bushes.*

*Always have a way to extinguish the fire quickly and completely.*

*Never leave a fire (even a cigarette) unattended.*

*Obey fireworks ordinances.*

If you're interested in doing more to prevent and fight fires, consider the following volunteer opportunity:

- Join a volunteer fire department. There are still far more volunteer firefighters in America than there are paid professionals, especially outside large cities. ⚹

## DISASTERS

The communication and safety plans for different types of disasters include important variations. Be sure to prepare for disasters that are common in your area. Most disasters happen suddenly; advance planning to minimize hazards can save serious injury and life. Here are a few things everyone can do to make a difference:

*Prepare for earthquakes:*

*Secure shelves, light fixtures, and water heaters.*

*Store heavy objects low, glass in cabinets with latches, heavy pictures and mirrors away from beds and couches.*

*Find safe places in rooms (under sturdy furniture, against an inside wall, away from windows) and outdoors (open areas away from buildings, trees, telephone and electrical lines, overpasses).*

*Prepare for tornadoes:*

*Stay tuned to weather information during thunderstorms: "tornado watch" means conditions are ripe for tornadoes; "tornado warning" means a tornado has already been sighted by radar.*

*Find safe shelter: below ground, lowest level of a building interior without windows, center of a room, under heavy furniture (never remain in a car or mobile home).*

*Prepare for hurricanes, tsunamis, and volcanoes:*

*Listen to weather information. (For hurricanes and tsunamis, know the height of your street above sea level and the distance from the coast.)*

*Be ready to evacuate. Make arrangements for pets, which are often not allowed in emergency shelters.*

*Plan two routes to higher ground; be ready to travel 20 to 50 miles.*

*Prepare for terrorism:*

> *Keep emergency items on each floor of multi-level buildings: battery operated radio, several flashlights, extra batteries, first-aid kit and manual, several hard hats.*

> *When the nation is "on alert," be watchful in large crowds and high-profile landmarks for unusual behavior, unattended packages, emergency exits, location of staircases, location of heavy and breakable objects that could fall or break in an explosion.*

> *Stay clear of areas surrounding suspicious packages during a bomb threat.*

> *Stay in your area after an explosion: cover your mouth with a handkerchief or clothing, tap on a pipe or wall so that rescuers can hear you. (Shout only as a last resort, since it causes inhaling dangerous amounts of dust.)*

> *Wait for instructions from local officials before donating food or clothing. They need time and facilities to be set up first for distribution or donations go to waste. Be prepared to deliver items.*

If you'd like to do more:

- Volunteer to help through agencies such as the Red Cross, Salvation Army, or local officials. ● ★ ♥ ⚔

---

*I have young grandchildren, so I signed up for a First-aid/CPR class at the local Red Cross chapter, just to brush up my skills. My course instructor happened to be an emergency services leader and he suggested I sign up for courses to become trained for disaster response. I guess you could say the rest is history.*

*Hurricane Andrew [in South Florida] was my first national assignment. Before this year, that was maybe the worst disaster I'd responded to.*

*—Bob Heintzelman, volunteer and assistant manager of a Red Cross service center near Ground Zero, New York*

## Training

The federal government anticipates that professional responders may be unavailable to help people in neighborhoods right after major disasters because of widespread destruction and the enormous need. There are, however, a variety of training programs available to those who would like to volunteer help during times of disaster. Volunteers with training are needed in the following areas:

> *From my stations, I got to talk to many of the families that came for help. . . . We were doing compassion and companion work, as well as feeding them. Some needed just a touch, while others needed me to sit and talk awhile, which I was glad to do.*
>
> *Disaster volunteering teaches me flexibility (during a relief operation, every day is different), the art of give and take, and how to make a team out of people who have never worked together before.*
>
> —Cheri Lundblad, Red Cross volunteer

- Cardiopulmonary resuscitation (CPR) and First aid ● ♥ ★

- Community Emergency Response Team (CERT): disaster preparedness, disaster fire suppression, disaster medical operations (2 units), light search and rescue, disaster psychology, CERT team organization

- The American Red Cross offers the following disaster courses free of charge: ● ♥ ★

  Introduction to disaster

  Family services

  Damage assessment

  Mass care

  Shelter operations

  Logistics overview and simulation

  Emergency response vehicle

  Family well-being inquiry

  Serving the diverse community

Records and reports

Emergency operations center

Other volunteer opportunities include:

- Emergency Response (Requires fifty-three hours of training; a college pre-Emergency Medical Technician course is now being offered to high school students in most states.)

- Emergency Medical Technician (EMT) (Requires 150 to 200 hours of training. Many volunteer fire fighters are also EMTs.)

- Search and Rescue (SAR) workers (Volunteers without training often join search and rescue organizations during an emergency. Volunteers may choose to become certified by obtaining extensive training at their own expense. Trained SAR workers may serve by offering training to committed volunteers at affordable costs.)

- Senior Corps or AmeriCorps (The Corporation for National and Community Service hopes to mobilize more than 15,000 participants to support police departments, fire departments, and other local agencies in assisting with public safety and disaster preparedness.)

- Amateur radio operators (Provide emergency communication for agencies and individuals when normal channels are down. Requires licensing.) ⚹

*When something exciting like a search happens, lots of people want to join up. As they find out what is required of them, many will drop out. Some just get bored and quit because there isn't always something "hot" happening. Each time we ride that roller coaster, the team will usually pick up a few "core" people to help make the group stronger. These individuals usually become part of a solid core group that can be counted on to do whatever is needed.*

*—Steve Foster, search and rescue team, Burke County, North Carolina*

## Internet Resources

Federal Emergency Management Agency (exhaustive material on disaster preparedness)
www.fema.gov

Learn CPR (a site with information and training resources)
http://depts.washington.edu/learncpr/

## Organizations

Contact your local fire department for CPR and CERT training. Contact your local chapter of the American Red Cross for CPR/First-aid training and Emergency Response and Disaster courses. (The American Red Cross has no minimum age requirements for their courses.)

American Red Cross
National Headquarters
430 17th St., NW
Washington D.C. 20006
800–448–3543
800–GIVE–LIFE (to give blood)
www.redcross.org

National Fire Academy
National Emergency Training Center
16825 S. Seton Ave.
Emmitsburg, MD 21727–8998
800–238–3358, ext. 1035
www.usfa.fema.gov/nfa/tr_emi.htm

National Association of Emergency Medical Technicians
P. O. Box 29233
Columbus, OH 43229
614–888–4484
www.naemt.org

National Association for Search and Rescue
4500 Southgate Place, Suite 100
Chantilly, VA 20151–1714
703–222–6277
www.nasar.org

# FOSTER CARE
# AND ADOPTION

*Save the children. Too many suffer and weep. God bless us to be mindful of them, to lift them and guide them as they walk in dangerous paths . . . to keep them secure until they can run with strength of their own.*

—Gordon B. Hinckley

No service is needed more than that given to the approximately half million children in foster care. Foster children need love, understanding, and experience in an average American family. Foster parents need training, support, and appreciation from mainstream society. Everyone can make a difference to foster children and their host families by understanding that:

- ● Groups
- ♥ Families
- ★ Youth
- ♥ Professional Qualifications
- ♀ Training Required

> *Foster children have had unfair disadvantages already in life. 75 percent of children are placed in foster care because of substance or alcohol abuse in their homes, 30 percent have emotional problems, and 58 percent have health problems (Child Welfare League of America, foster care fact sheet, October 1995).*

> *Foster parents are grief counselors and skilled disciplinarians.*

> *Children face separation issues no matter how difficult their home life was.*

> *Parents must be consistent and constructive, enforcing a few, clearly stated rules.*

## How to Help Foster Children

Volunteers are needed to:

- Be a foster parent family. Eligible individuals must receive thirty-two hours of training, receive first-aid and CPR certification, be between the ages of twenty-one and sixty-five, have a high school diploma, and be literate in English. There is a limit of six children per couple (including one's own) and four for a single person. Background checks are run on everyone living in the household. ♥ ⚧

- Be a temporary provider of emergency foster care. This involves providing immediate foster care for a maximum of ten days. ♥ ⚧

- Serve as a crisis/help line care provider. This involves a willingness to accept children placed by police during off-hours, such as nights and weekends. ♥ ⚧

- Be a specialized/structured foster care provider. These providers care for children who require increased care due to severe emotional, behavioral, or developmental problems and must have one year of foster care parenting experience. ♥ ⚧

- Prepare gifts for foster children to receive and give away—for birthdays, Mother's Day, Father's Day, the holiday season—and deliver them to foster care agencies. ● ♥ ★

---

*Disremembered and unaccounted for, she cannot be lost because no one is looking for her, and even if they were, how can they call her if they don't even know her name. Although she has claim she is not claimed. . . .*

—Toni Morrison, former foster child, author, and Nobel prize winner

---

### Sharing the Load

Studies show that 40 percent of foster families leave fostering in the first year of being licensed. The two largest reasons are role confusion or lack of support from the agency and lack of respite care. Families willing to foster children need help. Foster parents may trade kids informally during the week to allow each other some free hours. If you don't have the energy needed to volunteer as a foster parent, you may want to consider volunteering to help foster parents and foster care agencies share the load. Private foster care agencies welcome help from volunteers to:

*Statistics on Foster Care*

- *78 percent of children in out-of-home care live with foster families: 46 percent are Black, 38 percent White, 13 percent Hispanic.*
- *Children average 17 months in care (those leaving have been in about 11 months and those remaining have been in about 22 months).*
- *Two-thirds of children in foster care go back to the family or a relative within two years.*
- *Age of children when removed from homes: 29 percent are less than a year old, 42 percent are one to five years old, 23 percent are six to ten years old.*
- *Greatest needs: families of color, room for sibling groups, acceptance of emotionally disturbed teens and medically fragile/complex infants.*
- *65 percent of children adopted out of foster care are adopted by former foster parents (85 percent of these receive adoption subsidies).*

- Assist office staff. ● ★
- Mentor foster parents. ● ♥
- Provide relief care. ♥ ⚷ ]
- Be a "foster friend." Foster friends volunteer with agencies to befriend foster children or assist specific foster families as recommended by a caseworker.
- Tutor students. ★
- Assist with special events (such as luggage drives and book drives). ● ♥ ★
- Help with recruitment and provide training support.
- Develop a resource library.
- Assist with activities for foster children while their parents are receiving training. ● ♥ ★
- Help manage volunteer programs and student internships.

- Make up infant care kits (diapers, formula in zippered bags, etc.). ● ♥ ★

> The reward of foster care is loving a child who might never have been loved. We have seen a child hold his arms out, not knowing what it is like to be hugged. The children may go back to a situation that is not the best. They may end up in the foster care system again. But hopefully they will remember the year or eighteen months in a home where they were loved and hold onto it in the future.
>
> —Kris and Robert Weeks, foster parents

Another way to help is through teen independent living programs. All youth sixteen years and older who are still in state guardianship are entitled to participate in a whole range of living skill services to prepare them for a healthy and productive adult life. Volunteers are needed to:

- Assist youth with life-experience training (for example, teaching them how to fill out job applications and rental agreements, obtain bank accounts and drivers licenses, and work toward college scholarships). ● ♥

- Make up Independent Living Kits (a hamper filled with kitchen and laundry items, cleaning supplies, and so on) for youth heading out on their own. ● ♥ ★

## Adoption

Developing sensitivities to adoption issues is a significant service for a growing number of people in today's society. Everyone can make a difference by understanding that:

> Birth parents who become pregnant at the wrong time typically make an adoption plan for their child out of love.

> Adoption is an equally valid way to build families; families are legal institutions connected as well by love and commitment as blood.

> There are neither "real" nor "fake" parents. Adoptive parents are the real parents; they are the ones parenting. Birth parents may or may not be part of the picture.

> Children adopted internationally or interracially may or may not

*have any memory of their pasts. Don't ask if they are foreign.*
*The child is American. Children adopted internationally by*
*U.S. citizens automatically become U.S. citizens (effective 17*
*February 2001, retroactively).*

*School or church assignments that require a "family tree," baby*
*pictures, or genetic information may need adaptation. Trees*
*can have roots, everyone can bring a picture of when they*
*were younger; genetic exercises can be broadly based.*

---

*Our older son rushed to me and said in a cracked voice, "Mommy, we can't take the*
*baby; it will hurt them too much." And I turned to the birthmother and said, "Elliott*
*is afraid that we shouldn't take the baby because it will hurt you. Can you please tell*
*him what you want us to do?" And she—bless her wonderful heart—turned to him*
*with tears streaming down her face and said, "Baby, we need you to take him and*
*be his brother. Will you please do that for us?"*

*—Rebecca Walker, adoptive mother*

---

## How to Help

Some adoption agencies use outside volunteers (who must
sign a confidentiality agreement and undergo a background
check) to do the following:

- Answer phone calls from birth mothers and adoptive parents. ⚹
- Drive birth mothers to and from appointments.
- Make Birth Mother Healing Boxes (for women who make adoption plans for their babies). ● ♥ ⚹

There are a variety of adoption support groups that use volunteers to:

- Promote adoption awareness through community activities.
- Make adoption presentations to secondary schools. ⚹
- Share information on community services to women in need.

## MORE IDEAS FOR EXPANDING SERVICE

If you want to facilitate adoptions and foster care service in your area, here are some questions that may help you come up with a great volunteer opportunity:

- Is there a "no-cost outlet" for foster children and foster parents where they can select gifts, especially during the holiday season?

- Is there an organization in your area to help foster kids who are no longer wards of the state (ages eighteen through twenty-one)?

- Are there foster and adoptive-family support classes taught in your area, including something for grandparents and classes for couples waiting to be approved and parents who want more training?

- Do the hospitals in your area provide newborn-care classes for couples who are adopting or providing foster care for infants?

- Could you make blankets (to be distributed by local social workers and nurses) for pregnant young women who need help?

---

*She said, "How wonderful." Here it comes, I thought. How wonderful you are for adopting these children. All adoptive parents know how inappropriate that feels. But she didn't say that at all. "How wonderful," she said again, adding, "that you all found each other."*

*—Deborah C. Joy, adoptive parent and adoption therapist*

---

# Suggested Reading

Conna Craig and Derek Herbet, "The State of the Children: An Examination of Government-Run Foster Care." Available from the National Center for Policy Analysis, 655 15th St. NW, Suite 375, Washington D.C. 20005

Vincenette Scheppler, *Professional Parenthood: A Guide for Foster Care* (an excellent reference available on the Internet at www.arvinpublications.com for $3.00)

## Internet Resources

National Adoption Center: AdoptUSKids (pictures and descriptions of
children waiting for adoption)
www.adoptuskids.org

Survivors of the System: Foster Children United (a large resource for foster children and parents as well as the general public, developed by a
former foster child)
www.sos-fosternet.org

The National Adoption Information Clearinghouse
www.calib.com/naic/pubs/s_foster.htm

---

*Why am I doing this? Why, when I can't find enough time to sit down and read the
paper, am I giving my time to fostering? I got my answer last weekend. It was just
another crazy Saturday, I was trying to cram everything we didn't do all week into
one day and still have time to do the "family thing." I'm not sure how I ended up in
the grocery store on a Saturday but there I was, marching in line with hundreds of
faces.*

*When our eyes met we both looked startled for a split second and then came the
smiles. We stood for a few minutes just laughing and hugging. This beautiful, smiling
black woman and I had shared a child, from the age of four weeks. For over two
years we raised our little boy together, foster parent and birth mother. That has connected us forever. I know this woman's soul and she, mine. It's hard to get back to
melons and toilet paper after a moment like that.*

*—Anonymous foster parent*

---

## Organizations

Use the white pages to contact your local volunteer center for
adoption agencies and foster care organizations. Contact the
local children's service society to volunteer and donate Birth
Parent Healing Boxes.

Casey Family Programs (resources for foster children and families)
1300 Dexter Ave. North
Seattle, WA 98109
206–282–7300
www.casey.org

Child Welfare League of America (information on foster care and
    adoption)
440 First St., NW, Third Floor
Washington D.C. 20001–2085
www.cwla.org

Families Supporting Adoption (a support group of The Church of Jesus
    Christ of Latter-day Saints)
10 E. South Temple, Suite 1200
Salt Lake City, UT 84133
800–453–3860, ext. 7822

National Association of Foster Care Reviewers (lists local offices)
4665 Lower Roswell Rd., Suite 156
Marietta, GA 30068
www.nafcr.org

National Council for Adoption (guidelines and lists for choosing an
    agency or attorney)
225 N. Washington St.
Alexandria, VA 22314–2561
703–299–6633
www.ncfa-usa.org

National Foster Parent Association (lists local offices and opportunities
    to serve)
7512 Stanich Ave. #6
Gig Harbor, WA 98335
253–853–4000 or 800–557–5238
www.nfpainc.org

# GENEALOGY

*There is a moral and philosophical respect for our ancestors, which elevates the character and improves the heart.*

—*Daniel Webster*

Alex Hayley stirred the American mind to examine its past, not for noble pedigree but for powerful character. Current genealogical researchers are busy examining passenger lists, vital records, censuses, land and military records, slave records, and prison records for bits of information that will gradually create viable ancestral records. Most libraries have a genealogical department and, more recently, genealogy has become part of academic disciplines—serving sociology, genetics, and law. Genealogy is the link that will ultimately tie humankind together. It provides an invaluable service to living family members and future generations. It also keeps alive the memories of those who have passed on before us. Everyone can make a difference to his or her own family's history by:

● **Groups**
♥ **Families**
★ **Youth**
♥ **Professional Qualifications**
Ⴤ **Training Required**

*Keeping a family record—include children, siblings, parents, grandparents, extended family*

*Collecting or duplicating records of older family members before they are no longer available*

*Being willing to share records with other family members.*

## Getting Started

- Identify and record the following information about your family members: ♥ ★

  Full names (type or print surnames in all caps for easy scanning; remember to record maiden names for females)

  Birth dates and places (list dates by day, month, and year: 07 Jan 1855)

  Marriage dates and places (list places by city/township, county, state, country: Mesa, Maricopa, Arizona, USA)

  Death dates and places

  Place of burial

  Military service

  Interesting stories

*Genealogy allowed me to be able to step into the past and to feel what [my ancestors] had gone through, and to know that they tried tremendously to survive. To be able to know who my ancestors are, is not to bring shame to what they were, it is to elevate them to what they made possible for the generations after them.*

—Char McCargo Bah, family genealogist

It is easiest to record what you gather on pedigree charts and family group records, which are forms with spaces for names, dates, and places. You may also record information on a wide variety of computer programs. For example, new genealogy management software includes a Palm OS application and the ability to view user screens in six languages and enter data in most known languages, allowing users to take their data with them (without carrying printed reports or laptops) when doing family research away from home.

- Explore records. ● ♥ ★

Compiled/unofficial records include:

Obituaries

Biographies

Family histories

Family Bibles

Library genealogical files

Local historical societies

Internet files

Original/official records include:

Census records

Vital records (birth, marriage, death)

Probate records (wills)

Land records

Cemetery records

Immigration records

Naturalization records

Military records

As you look through official records, keep in mind that early census records have substantially less information than more recent records. Since 1790, the United States census has been taken every ten years. Census records, however, are made public seventy-two years later. Thus, the 1930 census was released in 2002. It is best to start with the most recent census records available and work your way back. Substantial records from the 1890 census were destroyed by fire.

The port of New York at Ellis Island, through which 40 percent of the United States population can trace one or more of their ancestors, has a new interactive computer center available to the public online with information on 22 million immigrants (see www.ellisislandrecords.org/).

- Document every bit of information you collect (even a listing of unproductive searches will be invaluable). ♥ ★

- Organize information. Be sure to select a system that works for you, whether it be numbering pedigree charts, alphabetizing surnames for family group records, or entering computer data. ● ♥ ★

## FAMILY INVOLVEMENT

Genealogy may be as much about understanding relatives as finding them. Family trees include the present and the past. Joining living generations plays a significant role in generating enthusiasm to link generations of the past. The inter-generational appeal of family history may be what is making genealogy a favorite pastime as well as a significant service for modern Americans. Family projects enhance and amplify search efforts. Consider one of the following projects:

> *Too often genealogists can get caught up in "just the facts." I think these invaluable family stories put life and character into these facts, without which it is all just an academic exercise. I took my video camera with me when I went to interview my 93-year-old great-aunt. She was the last surviving member of her generation. Not only did I get stories and info from two and three generations ago, I also have a wonderful remembrance of her.*
>
> *—Maureen Reed, author of "A Genealogy Primer"*

- Make a family heritage album. Include heirloom photos or color photocopies. Title the pages in your own handwriting. Write down ancestors' stories. Include newspaper clippings, old letters, certificates, ribbons, even locks of hair.

- Visit the cemeteries where your ancestors are buried. Make tombstone rubbings and take photographs (even granite stones may be hard to read a hundred and fifty years later). Leave flowers on Memorial Day, Veteran's Day, and other holidays.

- Celebrate an ancestor's birthday. Include food, music, and current events from the place and time where they lived.

- Hold a family reunion. Include storytelling about fore-bears, look-alike contests of ancestors, favorite recipes of Aunt B., a fashion show of grandchildren modeling grandparents' old clothes, and so on.

- Collect oral histories. Visit aging relatives with a tape recorder or video camera. Ask questions: What is your earliest memory? What was your life like when you were my age?

- Contribute to family newsletters.

## SHARING INFORMATION

The quickest way to make progress in genealogical research is to connect with someone further along and more experienced. Genealogy is not about competition; it is about communication. Hard-earned original research is magnified by sharing. Here are some ways to share what you find, and thus provide a valuable service to every member of your family:

> *I just feel it's very important to know who our ancestors were. Looking at a signature wasn't enough for me. I had to make connection to where this man [my great-grandfather] lived and where he died.*
>
> *—Alex Woodle, searcher of Ellis Island records*

- Submit your collection of family data to genealogical societies (be sure to determine the format each society requires for submissions).

- Connect with genealogical Web sites, many of which have a variety of services to assist people in finding others with similar research interests. Many Web sites facilitate collaborative E-mail lists and the creation of new E-mail listings concerning a specific ancestor or research topic.

- Create your own genealogical Web site.

Many nationwide projects, including the USGenWeb Archives Project (see www.usgenweb.org/projects/projects.html), are dedicated to putting actual transcriptions of public domain records on the Internet. Volunteers are needed for this and other projects to:

- Locate records.

- Transcribe information, including the U.S. federal censuses for free online use.

- Publish genealogical data. ⚹

- Help new users learn research skills.

- Adopt state and county Web pages and upload documents collected in research.

- Walk cemeteries and donate copies of the surveys to the archives. ♥ ●

- Transcribe pension-related materials for all wars prior to 1900.

- Develop lesson plans on genealogy for grades K-12. ❦

- Translate international genealogical Web pages. ⚹

- Take photos of tombstones or look up public records locally for people in other cities, states, or countries.

---

*You have to remember that the birth and christening records usually included the parents of the child. Marriage records often included the parents of the bride or the groom. With 4.5 million of these vital records [in the index for Scandinavia], the total number of individuals available in the database could easily be over 10 million. Imagine finding two or three generations of your ancestors from the 19th century or earlier at the click of a button from the convenience of your home.*

*—Paul Nauta, communications manager, The Church of Jesus Christ of Latter-day Saints, family and church history department*

## MORE IDEAS FOR EXPANDING SERVICE

The future of genealogy in health care and disease research is limitless. Scientists can learn about genetic trends from a vast accumulation of medical histories, abundant in families and organizations with extensive genealogical records. The records are used to link individuals together in family trees based on unique "markers" in their DNA. To help with molecular genealogy projects, watch for news articles and advertisements requesting participation. Brigham Young University in Provo, Utah, conducts one program in which volunteers give a blood sample and submit a four-generation biological pedigree chart.

## Suggested Reading

Cyndi Howells, *Netting Your Ancestors: Genealogical Research on the Internet*, Baltimore, MD: Genealogical Pub. Co., 1997.

Jim and Terry Willard, *Ancestors: A Beginner's Guide to Family History and Genealogy*, Boston: Houghton Mifflin, 1997.

Ralph Crandall, *Shaking Your Family Tree*, 2d ed., Boston: New England Historic Genealogical Society, 2001.

## Internet Resources

Ancestry.com (with a monthly subscription, users can access the 1790 through 1930 censuses online)
www.ancestry.com

Cyndi's List (a complete list of educational resources and genealogical classes)
www.cyndislist.com

Ellis Island (includes the names of people who immigrated between 1892 and 1924, as well as historical timelines)
www.ellisisland.org

Genealogy.com (online genealogy classes)
www.genealogy.com/university.html

The How-to Genealogy site (short descriptions of old handwriting deciphering and tombstone rubbings)
www.amberskyline.com/treasuremaps

International Internet Genealogical Society Translation Team (looking for volunteer translators)
www.iigs.org

Molecular Genealogy Research Group
http://molecular-genealogy.byu.edu

Random Acts of Genealogical Kindness (links volunteers around the world)
www.raogk.org

RootsWeb (extensive resources, focused on information sharing)
www.rootsweb.com

The United States Internet Genealogical Society (needs volunteer assistance with projects)
www.usigs.org

USGenWebProject (needs volunteer assistance transcribing census and tombstone records and with pension projects)
www.usgenweb.org

WorldGenWeb (needs Web masters throughout the world)
www.worldgenweb.org

## Organizations

Family History Library (the world's largest collection of genealogical information, links to 3,575 family history library branches in 65 countries; run by The Church of Jesus Christ of Latter-day Saints)
35 N. West Temple St.
Salt Lake City, UT 84150–3400
801–240–2331
www.familysearch.org

National Genealogical Society
4527 17th St. North
Arlington, VA 22207–2399
703–525–0050 or 800–473–0060

# HEALTH

*A wise man should consider that health is the greatest of human blessings, and learn how by his own thought to derive benefit from his illnesses.*

—Hippocrates

The health of a nation depends on the health of individuals. Those who are fit, healthy, and alert are better able to serve others and make viable contributions to their families, communities, and world. You can easily make a difference by focusing on wellness, self-care, and health preservation. Maintaining a healthy weight with diet and exercise decreases the risk of heart disease, diabetes, cancer, breathing problems, arthritis, reproductive complications, gall bladder disease, and depression. Other health benefits include mobility, physical endurance, and self-efficacy through the aging process. Everyone who maintains a healthy lifestyle helps the health of the nation. To make a difference:

| | |
|---|---|
| ● | Groups |
| ♥ | Families |
| ★ | Youth |
| ♥ | Professional Qualifications |
| ⚕ | Training Required |

*Build physical activity into regular routines. Adults should get thirty minutes of moderate physical activity most days of the week. Children should get at least sixty minutes.*

*Eat reasonable portions of a balanced diet with plenty of water.*

*Develop and share the attitude, skills, and confidence to stay active throughout life.*

## Community Health Service Opportunities

A third of Americans lack health care (see Edward J. Sondik, "Setting Priorities for the Delivery, Quality, Measurement, and Coverage of Clinical Preventive Services," Clinical Preventive Services Progress Review, National Center for Health Statistics: Healthy People 2000, Hyatsville, MD, 20 January 1998). The void in available health care leaves open a wide variety of volunteer positions in which professionals and concerned individuals can make up the difference in community education and service through organizations committed to improved health. Volunteer opportunities may include:

> *The people who come to the Fourth Street Clinic are so appreciative. Many are transient. I can freeze off warts, even treat skin cancer, but rashes like psoriasis or bad acne need expensive medications and require follow-up. Once in a while I have them come up from the clinic to my office. But because of insurance law and government regulations, they are legally required to fill out many papers which say they are indigent, so I can treat them for free. . . . But a lot can't get to the office or they get discouraged with the process. I could more easily do pro bono work when I had my private practice.*
>
> —*Marc Sanders, M.D. dermatologist*

- Educating people about heart disease ● ⚕
- Teaching children in schools and daycare settings how to avoid asthma attacks (present lessons; training provided by the American Lung Association) ⚕
- Educating people on the dangers of smoking; helping smokers to break the habit (present sessions; training provided by the American Lung Association) ⚕
- Teaching first-aid and CPR ♥
- Teaching community HIV and AIDS prevention classes ⚕
- Screening health records and doing intake on immunizations ⚕

The following health professionals are needed to serve in a variety of ways:

- Nurses: to give blood pressure clinics and administer immunizations and flu shots.

- Dentists, hygienists, and dental assistants: to provide restorative and prosthetic services at clinics for the homeless.

- Doctors with all kinds of specialties—surgeons, podiatrists, general practitioners: to give free services at clinics for the indigent as well as submit projects for private health organizations to study.

- Nutritionists: to conduct nutrition classes at aging centers.

- Physical fitness experts: to lead exercise classes in community centers.

- Health educators: to present classes for the elderly.

Nearly every community is looking for volunteers to give basic service in some of the following ways:

> *Eighty percent of people will need a blood product before reaching age seventy, but less than 4 percent of eligible donors choose to donate.*

- Give blood. Whole blood donations collected at blood drives can be separated into three components—red cells, platelets, and plasma—to help burn patients, cancer patients, victims of traumatic injuries, and those undergoing open heart surgery. Giving blood takes about thirty minutes. Platelets (the blood component that activates clotting needed for organ and bone marrow transplants and other critical medical treatments) are collected only in special blood centers. Platelet donation requires seventy minutes to two hours of your time. ●

- Register as a potential marrow or blood stem cell donor. This entails filling out a questionnaire and giving a small blood sample to determine your tissue type. (Donations from matched marrow donors are used to cure blood disorders such as leukemia and aplastic anemia.) ♥

- Participate in bona fide health studies that benefit society by providing more effective prevention and treatment of disease. ● ♥

- Encourage and assist people recently released from the hospital through the healing process. You can do this by making short visits, providing music and tapes, relieving a caregiver for a few hours, or simply offering a listening ear. ♥ ★

- Become a formal cancer volunteer. Offer encouragement to people in treatment by visits, phone calls, and E-mail. Cancer survivors must wait a year after treatment to apply, yet they are some of the most effective volunteers. To volunteer, contact cancer treatment centers and cancer wellness clinics. Breast cancer survivors may contact their local American Cancer Society chapters. ♥ ★

- Help the chronically ill. Be aware of neighbors, family members, and friends who struggle with chronic asthma, high blood pressure, arthritis, or diabetes. Encourage them with their daily health regimens. Check in regularly. Lend a hand on a bad day. Call and send letters if living away from a chronically ill family member. Volunteer with an organization that provides instruction and support. ● ♥ ★

- Find out if your community has a nursing service and volunteer through that organization. You could do a variety of things, including giving respite to caregivers of the terminally ill and administering immunizations for children in a "Care-A-Van" program. The following link will help you find a similar program in your community: www.national.unitedway.org/myuw/ ♥

- Contact your county's Division of Aging Services. They most likely need nurses, podiatrists, nutritionists, physical fitness experts, and health educators to perform services and/or conduct classes. ♥

- Volunteer with your county health department to teach food handler's permit classes or counsel those at high risk or newly diagnosed for HIV or AIDS or offer any other services they recommend. ⚔ ❤

- Volunteer at a public clinic or charitable health ministries to do intake on immunization records and health records. ⚔

---

*In a matter of hours, the effects rippled out to touch virtually everyone in the city, or, for that matter, the world. . . .*

*. . . Vast triage and trauma centers were set up, medical workers rushed in from all around the city and surrounding counties, and New Yorkers lined up by the thousands to donate blood until there was no place to store it.*

—Jerry Adler, "Ground Zero, After the Attack: Horror and Heroes," Newsweek, 24 September 2001, 74–76

---

## SERVING THOSE WITH HEALTH RISKS

The allure of alcohol, tobacco, and other drugs have caused some of the largest health problems in society. You can help by simply understanding the facts about addictive substances:

*Alcohol is a central nervous system depressant (which only initially acts as a stimulant).*

*More than 150 medications interact harmfully with alcohol and make mature adults vulnerable to dangerous, even fatal reactions.*

*Nicotine is a drug equally harmful whether it is smoked, chewed, or snuffed.*

*The rewards of quitting tobacco are immediate; and within ten to fifteen years, the risk of cancer and heart disease is almost as low as that of a nonsmoker (although permanent lung damage may remain). (See "Smoking: It's Never Too Late to Stop," National Institute on Aging, Age Page at www.nia.nih.gov/health/agepages/smoking.htm.)*

*Drugs affect the brain in a variety of ways. For example, cocaine increases blood pressure, which can cause bleeding and*

*strokes; heroin stimulates a pleasure system that causes last-*
*ing addiction; barbiturates induce sedation and coma;*
*inhalants can permanently damage the brain, causing mem-*
*ory loss, imbalance, visual impairments, and changes in per-*
*sonality.*

*Seventy-five percent of drug users choose marijuana, which*
*impairs motor coordination and disrupts both short-term*
*memory and learning; effects persist long after the euphoria or*
*sleepiness have passed.*

- Once you understand the facts, help educate others in schools, corporate offices, community settings and so on. The Community Anti-Drug Coalitions of America will be able to help you direct your efforts. Contact them at www.CADCA.org. ● ♥ ★

- Help someone with a drinking problem:

  Stop all "cover ups." Do not make excuses or protect the person from understanding the full consequences of his or her acts.

  Time your intervention. The best time is after a problem, when the people involved are calm, sober, and can talk privately.

  Be specific. Tell the family member or friend that you are worried about his or her problem—use examples of how it causes other problems.

  State the results. Explain what you will do if the person won't get help. Don't make threats you aren't prepared to keep.

  Get help. Gather information in advance about treatment options. If the person is willing, call immediately for an appointment. Offer to go with them.

  If the person refuses to accept help, call a friend. Ask the friend to talk with him or her, following the same steps. A friend who has recovered from the problem may be particularly persuasive; but any person who is caring and nonjudgmental may be effective.

The intervention of more than one person, more than one time, is often necessary.

Find strength in numbers. Some families join with other relatives and friends to confront the person as a group, but this is *only* advisable with the help of a health care professional.

Get support. It is important to remember that you are not alone. Understand that you are not responsible for the other person's problem. (From *Frequently Asked Questions on Alcohol Abuse and Alcoholism,* National Institute on Alcohol Abuse and Alcoholism, www.niaaa.nih.gov/faq/q-a.htm.)

## Internet Resources

American Alliance for Health, Physical Education, Recreation and
    Dance
http://aahperd.healthology.com

American Health Care Association (links to health and medicine sites)
www.ahca.org

Association for Integrative Medicine (holistic health and its service
    applications)
www.integrativemedicine.org

Centers for Disease Control and Prevention
www.cdc.gov

Community Anti-Drug Coalitions of America (5,000 local anti-drug
    coalitions)
www.CADCA.org

National Institute on Alcohol Abuse and Alcoholism (large resource on
    diagnosis and treatment)
www.niaaa.nih.gov

National Marrow Donor Program
www.marrow.org

Substance Abuse and Mental Health Services Administration
www.samhsa.gov

## Organizations

The American Red Cross provides volunteer opportunities to those who would organize blood drives, transport blood donations, teach CPR and first-aid classes, teach HIV and AIDS prevention, and so on. Look in your white pages to get phone numbers and addresses or on the Internet at www.redcross.org

The American Cancer Society, American Heart Association, American Lung Association, Easter Seals, United Way, etc. all have local offices which need volunteers to help in the office, teach classes, mentor individuals with illness, and so on. Look in your white pages to get phone numbers and addresses or check out their Web sites: www.cancer.org; www.americanheart.org; www.lungusa.org; www.easter-seals.org; www.unitedway.org.

Alcoholics Anonymous (AA: a twelve-step-to-recovery program so effective that more than one hundred other programs have been founded on the same principles.)
Contact a local office through your white pages.
www.alcoholics-anonymous.org

The Marrow Foundation
400 Seventh St., NW, Suite 206
Washington D.C. 20004
202–638–6601
www.themarrowfoundation.org

# THE HOMELESS: HUNGER AND HOUSING

*You don't have to be mean-spirited to walk away from social problems. All it takes is the certainty that nothing can be done to solve them.*

—*William Raspberry*

Hunger and homelessness rose sharply in the first year of the twenty-first century. Requests for emergency food climbed 17 percent. Over the same period of time, assistance rose only 12 percent. The great majority of American cities had to decrease the quantity of food provided at shelters

> ● **Groups**
> ♥ **Families**
> ★ **Youth**
> ♥ **Professional Qualifications**
> ⚡ **Training Required**

and/or the number of times families or individuals could come to obtain it (press release, 14 December 2000, United States Conference of Mayors).

As often as we may donate to food drives, support local shelters, or fix breakfast for people living under a viaduct, it is never enough. There is always more that can be done to help, and everyone can make a difference by simply doing the following things:

*Accept the homeless as fellow human beings.*

*Individualize expectations. Is the person temporarily jobless, substance addicted, lacking childcare, mentally ill?*

*Carefully study your options when giving assistance. Ask yourself:*

1. *Is giving a gift certificate, a box of granola bars, or some other tangible necessity better than giving money?*
2. *Is a cash handout feeding an addiction or a panhandling career?*
3. *Is not giving hand-outs my motivation to give to homeless charities?*

*Face root problems. Help at the source of the problem: counseling for multi-generational domestic violence; job training; solutions to low-income housing; help for mental illness.*

## FEEDING THE HUNGRY

Hunger remains a problem in America. Thirty-nine percent of the homeless go hungry some of the time. Twenty percent eat only once a day or less (see http://www. huduser.org/publications/homeless/homelessness/ch_3c.html for more results from the survey, *Homelessness: Programs and the People They Serve*). Men make up the majority of the adult homeless population. They have no place to store food, and they aren't allowed to stay in shelters during the day. The homeless are almost always on the move.

---

*Facts about the Homeless:*

- *The average age of a homeless person is low- to mid-30s.*
- *More than half have never married.*
- *38 percent abuse alcohol, 26 percent abuse drugs (the substance abusers die about 20 years earlier than the average American).*
- *A third to a half have chronic psychiatric disorders (schizophrenia, manic depression).*
- *30 percent have been jobless for more than two years.*
- *Most have lived in the same city for years.*
- *84 percent of homeless families are made up of single adult women with children—the largest growing segment of the homeless population.*
- *Average age of mothers is 27 (two-thirds of whom grew up in homes with alcohol, drugs, and abuse).*

Although food programs are often band-aids over much larger problems, it is hard to see anyone go hungry. To help, volunteers can:

- Give food through your church or a social service agency. They know where the real needs are.

- Give to food drives sponsored by reputable organizations such as the Boy Scouts, United States Postal Service, and food banks. Good food is never wasted. Food banks distribute through a wide variety of programs, including mobile food and outreach programs.

- Collect and transport goods to food banks and soup kitchens. ●

- Serve meals at your local soup kitchen. ● ★

## SHELTER

Two-thirds of the homeless use emergency shelters, transitional housing, or vouchers for emergency accommodations. The other third live on the streets (see ibid.). Shelters are always looking for volunteers, either on a one-time or ongoing basis. Most shelters are set up to accomodate groups of volunteers. The ideal group size is five to fifteen people. If you choose to volunteer, you might:

> *Our children just loved it. Even now, if we should happen to drive by one of those churches, they will say, "That's where we used to live!"*
>
> *—Theresa and Heriberto, recipients of Interfaith Hospitality*

- Take a shift at the shelter, serving food, washing dishes, sorting and distributing clothes. ● ♥ ★

- Staff the computer lab, teaching clients to type, helping them brush up on computer skills, or accommodating access to the Internet.

- Greet guests at the front desk and help with clerical work: answering phones, typing, filing, or sorting mail. Volunteers are especially needed in the summer months when college students are not so available. ★

- Conduct self-sufficiency programs. ☈

- Tutor youth and adults.

- Sponsor activities in the playrooms of family shelters. ● ♥ ★

- Share your hobby with groups in the shelter; ask about theirs.

- Invite people who are experiencing homelessness to a community event, such as a worship service, public concert, or picnic. (Note that there are important boundary issues you will be expected to follow—never invite someone you are serving in this capacity into your home). ● ♥ ★

- Offer hairstylist or barber services. ♥

- Provide birthday and holiday parties for shelter residents. ● ♥

- Entertain with music.

- Adopt a family for a holiday; prepare a food box for a family newly transitioned back into the community. ♥

- Help a homeless person make contact with family members, especially for holidays.

- Donate new or used clothing (underwear and diapers must be new), personal hygiene products, gift certificates, housewares, cleaning supplies, bedding, cribs, and so on to shelters.

- Volunteer with interfaith organizations that open their churches at night for homeless families: fix meals, chaperone over night, provide transportation. ●

Transitional housing programs exist in most cities and provide opportunities for people to make a more gradual adjustment between living in shelters and reaching full-scale independence. Such programs offer support so that people can heal and fortify themselves to start all over again. Most homeless people have been jobless longer than they have been homeless and have thus lost support systems. Among other things, transitional housing programs provide self-sufficiency instruction. Volunteers can help with:

- Job search seminars ⚉
- Presentations on self-esteem, skill building, and employment placement. A client may simply want to hear a volunteer talk about life experiences in the workplace and ask questions about resumes, interviewing, and the job market.
- Adopting a family during transition ♥
- Mentoring
- Tutoring and adult education

> *People want to help out but they don't want to see the problem. They're afraid their children are going to end up in school with homeless kids.*
>
> *We found an old warehouse out in the country to accommodate the overflow in the shelter—so that no one is forced into the cold during the winter. It opened with a two-year trial, approved for conditional use. The chief of police out there was so against it. Now it's become this great community love fest. People are always bringing in food and supplies and there has been no increase in crime.*
>
> *We have no idea what stranded people have been through. They come here with nothing. Some have lost hope because they've fallen so many times. We have case managers who help them make a plan. As long as they are working to achieve it they can stay as long as they like. We changed our name to The Road Home—that's our mission now.*
>
> —Caroline Alder, volunteer coordinator, The Road Home

## HOUSING

The Department of Housing and Urban Development has many programs for helping individuals who are homeless or who don't qualify for housing because of income requirements or disabilities. In addition many private, nonprofit organizations use volunteers to help fill growing housing needs. Housing programs require the recipients' commitment to specific goals in budgeting, credit repair, and savings. Volunteers can help recipients build their dreams and get into a home by:

- Supplying materials and employee time for construction and repairs of homes and apartments ●

- Supporting organizations that sponsor programs to upgrade a whole neighborhood ● ♥ ★

- Volunteering with Habitat for Humanity (www.habitat.org/) to pound nails, cut lumber, put up drywall, clean, sweep, and carry materials with people who need help in building their houses ● ♥ ★

- Volunteering with organizations like "Rebuilding Together" (www.rebuildingtogether.org/), which sponsors Christmas in April by repairing homes for the low-income elderly and people with disabilities ● ♥ ★

- Assisting through the Volunteer Center on Make a Difference Day (see www.usaweekend.com/diffday/) and United Way Day to fix up community shelters or some other community buildings and locations ● ♥ ★

> *The sweat equity I do is worth it because I am learning to take care of my own home. When I am in the other houses here that are almost finished, I imagine what it will be like to have my own home. I can hardly wait.*
>
> —*Tracye Bryant, single mother, Habitat for Humanity*

## COMPLEX PROBLEMS

Substance abuse and mental illness are among the most difficult problems to treat. Indifference to these growing problems is definitely not the solution. Anyone with a family member who gets hooked on alcohol or drugs or who develops bi-polar symptoms knows to marshal all the support they can find—both medically and socially—to change the trend. The homeless do not have family members to turn to for support when facing these problems. The rigors and dangers of street or shelter existence increase isolation among the homeless and place them in grave danger. Much help is required to provide the support these people need—to change if possible, or to endure their illnesses. Volunteers are needed to:

- Assist shelter staff, patiently. Providers are often under-funded and understaffed. Let staff members and directors know you can help, when and for how long, and then give them time to figure out how to work you in. As you stay on, you will understand the variety of assistance needed.

- Organize and distribute supplies (socks, underwear, hygiene kits) to groups that provide assistance to homeless drug addicts.

- Teach self-sufficiency skills.

To help the homeless in any capacity, contact community food banks, shelters, family support centers, substance abuse centers, outreach programs, housing authorities, and church-run programs for the homeless.

---

*It's a simple circle, but I think it has made a wonderful difference in many lives, including my own. I try to help the residents take advantage of and enjoy the computing resources, and they end up teaching me and reaching out to each other.*

*There are all types of people who use the lab. Some want to learn how to use the computer or how to type, some want to play a few games or surf the Internet, and several build their own web pages, search for jobs or check E-mail.*

*Of course the residents eventually move on, but I think that many of them will take with them new skills and confidence that they can then share with others.*

—Jonathan Ames, shelter volunteer

---

## Suggested Reading

Alice S. Baum and Donald W. Burnes, *A Nation in Denial: The Truth about Homelessness*, Boulder, Colo.: Westview Press, 1993.

## Internet Resources

Homelessness: Programs and the People They Serve
www.huduser.org/publications/homeless/homelessness/highrpt.html

National Coalition for the Homeless
www.nationalhomeless.org

## Organizations

Habitat for Humanity
121 Habitat St.
Americus, GA 31709
229–924–6935
www.habitat.org

National Alliance to End Homelessness (facts and volunteer ideas; lists
    of supporting government organizations)
1518 K St., NW, Suite 206
Washington D.C. 20005
202–638–1526
www.endhomelessness.org

National Interfaith Hospitality Network (churches providing shelter,
    meals, and assistance for people who are homeless)
71 Summit Ave.
Summit, NJ 07901
908–273–1100
www.nihn.org (provides a list of local networks in 35 states)

Neighborhood Reinvestment Corporation (sponsors NeighborWorks, a
    neighborhood revitalization and educational service)
1325 G St., NW, Suite 800
Washington D.C. 20005–3100
202–220–2300
www.nw.org

Points of Light Foundation (sponsors Make a Difference Day with
    Volunteer Centers)
1400 I St., NW, Suite 800
Washington D.C. 20005
202–729–8000
www.pointsoflight.org

Rebuilding Together with Christmas in April
1536 Sixteenth St., NW
Washington D.C. 20036–1402
202–483–9083 or 800–4–REHAB9
www.rebuildingtogether.org

The Salvation Army
615 Slaters Ln., P. O. Box 269
Alexandria, VA 22313–0269
703–684–5500
www.salvationarmyusa.org

Travelers Aid Society
1612 K St., NW, Suite 506
Washington D.C. 20006
202–546–1127
www.travelersaid.org

United Way of America
701 N. Fairfax St.
Alexandria, VA 22314–2045
703–836–7100
www.unitedway.org

Volunteers of America (services vary by area but include emergency care
    of the homeless population: Alcohol/Drug Detoxification Centers,
    Homeless Youth Resource Centers, employment and training, out-
    reach)
1660 Duke St.
Alexandria, VA 22314–3427
800–899–0089
www.voa.org

# HOSPITALS

*A merry heart doeth good like a medicine.*
—Proverbs 17:22

It is the personal touch that turns hospitals into healing environments. People with time for conversation and the desire to understand another's fear or pain or hope help patients to make it through the suffering and anxiety of a hospital stay. Everyone can make a difference to someone who is ill by:

- ● Groups
- ♥ Families
- ★ Youth
- ♥ Professional Qualifications
- ☧ Training Required

> *Visiting a family member or a friend in the hospital to communicate caring and support. The best visits are upbeat, reasonably short, and easygoing.*

> *Making house calls to patients recently released from the hospital and those with severe chronic illnesses.*

## CHOOSING A VOLUNTEER POSITION

Volunteer coordinators are always looking for people who will help during regular visiting hours on set days of the week—people who can make a commitment and keep it. Likewise, volunteer coordinators are discouraged by people who can't make a commitment and only show up sporadically. (Larger groups that entertain patients and host activities are the exception.) The rewards of regular service are great; individual volunteers become part of a team, almost like a family, and share the goal of a hospital's medical and administrative staff. Volunteers are a large part of what makes a hospital operate smoothly.

Hospital volunteers must take an annual TB test and may also be required to have a background check and proof of vaccination for hepatitis B. If you would like to volunteer at a hospital, it will be helpful to first observe others who are serving in a similar capacity. Make sure you know what is expected of you. Ask a lot of questions before committing to a position. Here are five questions to ask yourself as you decide what area of hospital service best suits your desires:

> Mr. Barnes was scheduled for abdominal surgery. He was anxious—scared of the unknown, the pain, and especially the strangers who would invade his body. A friend visiting him the night before surgery provided the solution. The next morning, Mr. Barnes arrived in the operating room grinning from ear to ear. Soon after the staff began preparing him for surgery, they started to laugh. On his belly they found a sticker requesting. "Hey, Doc, while you're in there could you check the oil?"
>
> After the surgeon completed Barnes's surgery, he placed a strip of tape on the bed with these words, "Oil checked, tires rotated. Next inspection tomorrow morning or 30,000 miles, whichever comes first."
>
> —in Allen Klein, Courage to Laugh (N.Y.: J.P. Tarcher/Putnam, 1998), 64.

1. Do you work better with children, adults, or the elderly?

2. Do you have experience with specific diseases, orthopedic disabilities, or chronic health challenges?

3. Do you want to work directly with patients, or would you be more comfortable working with medical records, phone inquiries, or family members in the waiting room?

4. Do you prefer a well-defined job, or are you content to look around for the people who need help?

5. Do you want to assist with an activity, or would you like to sponsor one?

## TYPES OF POSITIONS

Following is a list of areas in which you can volunteer at most hospitals. A brief explanation of coordinating responsibilities is also included:

- Lobby host: greet visitors, answer questions, give directions. ★

- Waiting rooms: answer questions, act as liaison between staff and families.

- Gift shops and snack bars: stock, serve, staff the cash register. ★

- Flower and mail delivery: retrieve and dispense items; meet patients. ★

- Emergency room: replenish supplies, check patients, help families of patients.

- Nursing floors: pass water and food trays, escort patients and visitors, visit, run errands. ★

- Clerical assistant: data entry, filing.

- Newborn nursery: assist nurses with babies.

- Outpatient clinics: assist with admittance, answer questions.

- Physical therapy: assist therapists, walk with ambulatory patients.

- Translation: interpret for patients.

- Family services: organize activities and entertainment. ● ♥ ★

- Child life: visit children, read stories, teach arts and crafts. ● ♥ ★

- Church volunteers: provide religious services, visit patients. ● ♥ ★

- Junior volunteers/high school interns: work in a variety of departments. ★

## CREATIVE EXPERIMENTS

Patch Adams, the doctor made famous in Robin Williams's movie of the same name, believes that people with serious illnesses are helped by being able to laugh. Many hospitals and care units are catching on to the "Patch Adams philosophy" that "all healing arts are welcome, all patients will be treated as friends and the health care experience will be infused with fun." Other creative people are experimenting with ways to appropriately lighten up hospital environments. Here are some ideas:

- Put together an art cart featuring framed posters. Help patients choose a piece of art they would like to hang in their rooms during their recovery. Encourage rotating art exhibits in hospitals. ●

- Assist patients in creating collages that symbolize the healing journey. Use objects from nature, personal memorabilia, paint, and so on. ● ★

- Facilitate patient expression through story writing. (Issues of growing in the face of health challenges often emerge.) ⚕

- Scribe for "told poems"; encourage the patient to tell you about his or her thoughts and record them in a free form on paper.

- Distribute scrapbooking supplies for patients and families to record their expressions with pictures and poems. ★ ●

- Offer to tape record a patient's life stories.

- Utilize sand trays, a natural tactile treat for child patients, and group exploration for adults. ⚕ ♥

- Sponsor hat days, where volunteers and staff wear fabulous hats. Offer hats to patients—make hats with soft linings for cancer patients who have lost their hair as a result of chemotherapy. ● ♥ ★

- Teach new skills to recovering patients; basket weaving, watercolor, lap quilting.

- Share skills in music, art, or dance therapy. Schedule performances of musical groups, acting or mime groups. ● ♥ ★ ♥

- Provide fabric squares for patients to design. Sew into a quilt for an award or auction. ● ♥ ★

- Compile a hospital book of healing stories from staff and patients that can enrich healing of others. ● ♥

- Create an alcove to display amulets, figurines, folk remedies, and other objects that tell healing stories in other cultures dominant in the patient population. ● ♥ ★

- Play a musical instrument. Perform as a musical group. In some hospitals it is especially important to include performers of Native American, Hispanic, or African music to please a culturally diverse clientele. ● ♥ ★

> *All my kids love coming here. While Riley is doing his physical therapy the others play in the activity area. I like the way volunteers gather us for activities—especially the puppet shows and the quilt making, which are fun even for me. It connects patients and their families when we're feeling kind of alone. This is a happy place— more like a home or a rec center than a hospital. Thank goodness—I've spent a big part of my life here during the last five years.*
>
> —Chantel Lloyd, *mother of a Shriners Hospital patient*

Volunteers in direct patient care should follow these twelve specific suggestions:

1. Always knock on a patient's door, whether open or closed.

2. Introduce yourself. Get permission to interact.

3. Encourage dialogue.

4. Stay positive. Focus on abilities, *not* disabilities.

5. Respect confidentiality.

6. Avoid providing false hopes.

7. Share personal information at your own discretion.

8. Restate any positive things that a patient says.

9. Be culturally sensitive; patient may not communicate in English.

10. Be sensitive to hearing loss; look directly at patient, speak distinctly using lower pitched tones, stay close, eliminate background noise.

11. Be sensitive to visual impairments; do not move objects without permission, identify new objects you are placing in the room, such as water, flowers, tissues.

12. Be sensitive to mobility limitations: patients may be unable to open food containers.

## VARIED HOSPITALS

Though most hospitals have the same basic needs, clientele and focus of care may vary greatly from location to location. Hospitals may be connected to medical and rehabilitation centers, even care facilities.

### Veterans' Affairs

Veterans' Affairs has the largest volunteer program in the federal government with at least one hospital facility in every state. They welcome youth ages twelve and up and offer award scholarships to exceptional student volunteers. Volunteers may learn to:

> They were always happy to see a young face. Volunteering has helped to complete me. When I lost my grandfather, I lost a piece of myself, but helping veterans created a new link.
>
> —Justin Gracely, youth volunteer turned physical therapy major

- Escort patients to and from appointments within the facility. ★
- Deliver medical charts. ★
- Take patients on walks to the library. ★
- Furnish and deliver birthday cards. ★
- Provide musical entertainment. ● ♥ ★
- Triage patients in the outpatient department. ⚢ ♨

- Computerize library files or set up an Access database.

- Explain health care eligibility to other veterans. ⚕

- Do patient evaluations in a rehabilitation unit. ⚕

- Teach an art class or a ceramics class.

- Assist in the stockroom. ★

- Read to patients—the newspaper, the Bible, jokes from *Reader's Digest*. ★

- Escort hospitalized veterans to church services. ♥ ★

- Transport patients to hospital facilities/take a veteran fishing. ♥

### Children's Hospitals

Children's hospitals depend on volunteers to assist with activities especially appealing to children and to accommodate their absence from regular school. A volunteer at a children's hospital might:

- Tutor children receiving long-term care. ★

- Make art murals along with patients, their families, even staff, to create permanent or temporary displays.

- Sew adaptive clothing for orthopedic patients, such as shorts that snap along the seams for patients in casts and leg lengthening devices.

- Make kids' bags and costumes for Halloween. Adapt a trick-or-treat experience to departments in the hospital. ● ♥ ★

- Offer art supplies to patients in their rooms—crayons, paints, drawing pads.

- Equip patients with artist tape (crepe-paper-based and backed with low-adhesive glue). The medium works on walls in intensive care units and isolation wards as well as patient rooms.

- Assist patients or family members in creating healing dolls from a plain stuffed doll, using fabrics and paints. ● ♥ ★

- Put on a short play or puppet show for patients, with family members as the cast.

- Clown with patients, using props such as mirrors, bubbles, and magnifying glasses. ⚹

- Grow a hospital garden. Involve patients and their families. Plant flowers, tomatoes, herbs. Bring flowers into patient rooms, make salsa for an activity. ● ♥ ★

- Be a special friend to foreign-speaking patients and their parents.

> *The murals make the children happy. The kids pretend they're in the jungle, so they sleep real good and wake up happy.*
>
> —*Rafeek, nine-year-old patient*

## Senior Care Facilities

Experiments in helping elder patients has generated programs such as "TOPA" (Towards Older Person Awareness) and "HELP" (Help Elder Life Program), where volunteers focus on individuals over the age of seventy during their hospital stay. These programs have already proven to diminish disorientation and delirium. Volunteers might be asked to:

- Visit seniors every day during their hospital stay.

- Create "almost home" programs, which sponsor activities such as yoga and adapted aerobics. ● ⚹

- Host beauty days—do facials, manicures, and take "after" photos. ★

## A HOSPITAL'S WISH LIST

Every hospital facility has a wish list of items that will help patients and bring joy into every room. Check with the hospital in your community for a list of the things they specifically need. You might be able to furnish some of the following:

- "Take-home" quilts for patients
- Lap quilts, comfort pillows (4" x 6")
- Comfort caps (simple caps of soft cloth for patients who have lost their hair during chemotherapy; consider making a few larger caps in fabrics suitable for men)
- Mementos for grieving families
- Art supplies
- Gift packages (homemade crafts or gift items for a specific holiday or season)
- Goody bags (contents not homemade)
- Seasonal decorations
- Scrapbook supplies for parents with premature babies
- Handmade cards that patients can send
- Hair care products for people in intensive care
- New underwear and T-shirts for children from low-income families

## More Ideas for Expanding Service

Some organizations focus on helping the families of hospital patients. For example, Ronald McDonald Houses throughout the country provide a place for families who want to stay while their children receive long-term care. The houses are located near hospitals that serve children. Families stay virtually free of charge, but the service is made possible through efforts of many volunteers. Volunteers at a Ronald McDonald House might be asked to:

- Answer phones
- Keep up the house and yard ● ♥ ★
- Prepare food

## Suggested Reading

Patch Adams, *House Calls*, San Francisco, Calif.: Robert D. Reed
    Publishers, 1998.

## Internet Resources

Arts and Healing Network (lists links to community art projects at hos-
    pitals and care facilities)
http://www.artheals.org/community/hosp/hosp.html

The Gesundheit! Institute
www.patchadams.org

## Organizations

Contact your local hospitals, medical centers, and rehabilitation centers for most volunteer opportunities.

Department of Veterans Affairs Voluntary Service (listed locally in the
    blue pages under U.S. government)
810 Vermont Ave., NW
Washington D.C. 20420
202–273–8952
www.va.gov/volunteer

Ronald McDonald House Charities
One Kroc Dr.
Oak Brook, IL 60523
630–623–7048
www.rmhc.com

# INTERNATIONAL

*Philanthropy might be divided into two roles: maximizing human potential and relieving human misery. Some of the best projects bridge the two.*
—Brian O'Connell

The revelation of all international associations is that people are so much alike. All people want safety, health, and opportunity for themselves and their children. Would-be helpers want to decrease suffering in the world, but global problems

● **Groups**
♥ **Families**
★ **Youth**
♥ **Professional Qualifications**
**ﾢ Training Required**

appear discouragingly large. Yet hope is sprouting around the world. The American dream is spreading abroad. People are grasping onto principles of self-reliance facilitated by other individuals who offer education, health assistance, and small amounts of venture capital. When people from different countries become acquainted, they learn from each other; and it changes them all. The instrument of progress is one-on-one interaction. Everyone can make a difference in the world by:

*Feeling personally the needs of the developing world.*

*Getting acquainted with refugee or immigrant neighbors.*

*Attending international art exhibits, music competitions, or sporting events.*

*Following the news to learn what others do to help during world emergencies; observe which organizations make significant contributions.*

## GETTING STARTED

Cultivating friendships with people abroad, personally or through an organized group, is an important step in international service. Volunteers can:

- House an international exchange student; sponsor yours or someone else's child. ♥

- Correspond with people from other countries; find a pen pal abroad. ♥ ★

- Support an international service organization (possibilities include church humanitarian and education organizations, Rotary International, Soroptimist International, Sister Cities, Kiwanis, and so on). ●

Timely service is usually not about starting a new organization but expanding the effectiveness of an existing group. Organizations need a lot of help at home in order to function abroad. You can:

> *I would rather have originated the Red Cross than to have written the constitution of the United States.*
>
> —*Will Rogers*

- Volunteer in the home office of an international humanitarian organization; assist with accounting, translation, publicity, Web site maintenance, and writing publicity articles. ★

- Educate people about other countries; give school presentations for an international organization about the part of the world they serve.

- Clean your closet and donate clothes to relief organizations (replace missing buttons). ♥ ★

- Collect donations.

- Make kits—sewing kits, school kits, hygiene kits, newborn kits. (Keep in mind that all kits must be made according to guidelines of the service organization with which you are working.) ● ♥ ★

- Sew/crochet hand towels, quilts, and tropical sore bandages. ● ♥ ★

- Sort and pack items for humanitarian organizations.

## Volunteer Vacations

Innumerable organizations worldwide have learned how to utilize "volunteers on vacation." These opportunities are for people who want adventure—there are no guarantees that the experience will be trouble free. People are wise to directly contact the organization in which they have particular interest; ask specific questions of staff, and interview previous volunteers. Volunteer vacations require enthusiasm, a desire to help, and good health. And, while many of them sound exotic, they can be physically draining. Some examples of the hundreds of volunteer vacations available include:

> *When we entered the village the elders were summoned by Talking Drum. We gathered inside the chief's hut on furs in 110-degree heat. "Thank you, thank you, thank you," said the chief again and again through translators. "Your visit is like gold to us." Then the chief, elderly and blind, described how life in the village had been changed by the school. Seventeen years ago anything written had to be carried by hand or bicycle to the city (an hour and a half away by car) for reading. Now, even the village children can read written materials.*
>
> —Martha Ethington, executive director of the Ouelessebougou-Utah Alliance

- Participating in sea turtle conservation on coasts around the Mediterranean ⚹
- Helping with archaeological excavations in Spain ⚹
- Documenting historic buildings in the Caribbean ⚹
- Running summer camps for children in Bosnia ♥ ⚹

## Expeditions

Some non-governmental organizations (NGOs) sponsor short-term expeditions to accomplish prearranged service projects. Much good can be accomplished in a concentrated time period when a group of people are working together to help a community accomplish larger or more technical goals than it can accomplish alone. To perpetuate the benefits, however, the local leaders must want the services and the local population must receive respect and support from visiting volunteers. Volunteers on an expedition might:

- Build a school room; provide teacher training and books.
- Conduct workshops in primary health care training; host a health clinic. ♥ ⚔
- Perform surgeries—cleft palate, cataract removal, gynecological problems. ♥
- Construct cisterns or water filtration systems.
- Build a greenhouse or construct an irrigation system.
- Build a medical facility.
- Take photographs; bring pictures home to educate.
- Write an article upon return.

> *One of the children who touched me the most was a six-year-old boy who had been burned in a cooking accident at the age of one. He had burns all over his body, most severe on his limbs. His one wish pre-operatively was to be able to clean himself. . . . As we removed the bandages, tears of joy flowed from his eyes. . . . It appeared that the surgery was a success, and that this little boy would have a working thumb and be able to hold a pencil, hold a spoon, and be able to clean himself.*
>
> —*Rex Matthews, Fourth-year medical student, Operation Smile volunteer*

## HUMANITARIAN MISSIONS

Humanitarian missionaries have a strong spiritual commitment to help their fellow beings. Drawn together by religious conviction, they share common values and work comfortably together toward shared goals. They are needed throughout the world to facilitate long-term local community projects. Humanitarian missionaries might:

- Pipe water into villages. ⚔
- Assist with health care: run a blood bank or teach neonatal resuscitation or eye care, for example. ♥

- Teach English, computer skills; help in local schools. ☧
- Assist with family agriculture; support animal husbandry and family food production. ♥ ☧
- Teach parenting classes.
- Assist with community agriculture; help with school gardens for healthy lunches.
- Give micro credit support; offer vocational training; teach sewing. ♥ ☧
- Enhance hospital care: set up an Activity Center for young cancer patients.
- Start a scout program for youth.
- Provide handicraft projects for senior citizens.
- Provide disaster relief for floods, famines, earthquakes, and so on.

## NGOs

Organizations that make substantial long-term commitments to third world countries reap the benefits. Some may focus on one area of the world, others have expanded to several. Organizational focus may vary—one group may develop expertise in agriculture, another in health or education, and then they may partner. Success is tied to long-term commitment and respect for local initiative. People working in a long-term program need special training (native language skills in many areas are essential). The Peace Corps, for example, has an excellent training program in language and culture, and their philosophy of "work yourself out of a job" is empowering to native people. Participants in NGOs:

> We teach English as an international language; there is no way Asians can achieve in commerce without it. Of course we make it free and fun—with songs and dances. Then we offer computer training so the students can get a job. The computer system is now linked to the university.
>
> —Daryl and Hank Hoole, humanitarian missionary senior couple

- Build friendships around sharing each others' culture.

- Teach literacy with practical applications, such as helping people learn to read a health manual. Expect to repeat instructions in oral cultures many times. ⚹

- Train local leaders in health care; let them become the experts. Beware of American gimmicks; local interest must exist to implement the use of anything new. (It may be "trendy" to teach natives how to can, for example, but that's not necessary if the natives prefer fresh food and have it available year round.) ⚹

- Facilitate local discussion; strive to understand all issues from the local point of view.

> *The villagers appreciate things in different proportions. I have to consider what work is, what recreation is. I can offend them by working too hard during the day. Seasons change everything. For them spending the afternoon sipping tea under a mango tree during the hot season is smart. Then they can work in the evening when the electricity is on and rise early to work in the fields. They ask themselves, "Why can Monica work an eight-hour day?" and they come up with, "She had vitamins growing up."*
>
> —Monica LaBelle, Peace Corps volunteer

## Suggested Reading

Bill McMillon, *Volunteer Vacations*, 8th ed., Chicago, Ill.: Chicago Review Press, 2002.

Louise Whetter and Victoria Pybus, eds., *The International Directory of Voluntary Work*, 7th ed., Beccles, Suffolk, England: William Clowes Ltd., 2001.

Joan Powell, ed., *Alternatives to the Peace Corps: A Directory of Third World Volunteer Opportunities*, 9th ed., Oakland, Calif.: Food First Books, 2000.

## Internet Resources

InterAction (lists 160 U.S.-based relief agencies and the world projects they are supporting)
www.interaction.org

International Tandem Network (connect via phone, E-mail, or other
medium with a friend from a foreign country)
www.slf.ruhr-uni-bochum.de/etandem/etindex_en.html

International Volunteering Programs
www.volunteerinternational.org

Linguistic Funland! (E-mail pen-pal opportunities for students)
www.linguistic-funland.com

American Red Cross (children learning about children abroad)
http://kidsfund.redcross.org

## Organizations

Contact church humanitarian organizations, your own faith,
and others.

ADRA International (Adventist world development and relief)
12501 Old Columbia Pike
Silver Spring, MD 20904
888–237–2367
www.adra.org

American Field Service
AFS Western States
310 SW 4th Ave., Suite 630
Portland, OR 97204–2608
800–AFS–INFO (For addresses and information about AFS in all states)
www.usa.afs.org

Beehive International (Christian charity seeking volunteers)
1101 W. Mermod
Carlsbad, NM 88220
505–885–2178

Brother's Brother Foundation (facilities worldwide distribution of books)
1200 Galveston Ave.
Pittsburgh, PA 15233–1604
888–232–1916
www.brothersbrother.org

CARE (emergency relief and long-term programs, volunteer expeditions)
151 Ellis St., NE
Atlanta, GA 30303–2440
800–422–7385
www.care.org

Catholic Relief Services
209 W. Fayette St.
Baltimore, MD 21201–3443
800–724–2530
www.catholicrelief.org

CHOICE: Center for Humanitarian Outreach and Inter-Cultural
    Exchange
7879 S. 1530 W., Suite 200
West Jordan, UT 84088
801–474–1937
www.choicehumanitarian.org

Citizens Democracy Corps (seeking volunteer business advisors)
1400 I St., NW, Suite 1125
Washington D.C. 20005
202–872–0933
www.cdc.org

Deseret International Foundation (seeking longterm medical specialists)
1282 E. Cambridge Ct.
Provo, UT 84604
801–489–1315
www.deseret-international.org

Doctors Without Borders (emergency medical care)
6 E. 39th St., 8th floor
P. O. Box 2247
New York, NY 10016
888–392–0392
www.doctorswithoutborders.org

Enterprise Mentors International (charity organization building self-
reliance)
16100 Chesterfield Pkwy West
Suite 395
Chesterfield, MO 63017–4873
800–829–9452
www.enterprise-mentors.org

Habitat for Humanity International
121 Habitat St.
Americus, GA 31709
229–924–6935
www.habitat.org

Humanitarian Resource Center of North America (accepts in-kind
donations and facilitates distribution)
1600 S. Empire Rd. #700
Salt Lake City, UT 84104
801–977–0444
www.relieffund.org

Latter-day Saint Charities (various kits and donations opportunities
worldwide)
50 E. North Temple St., 7th Floor
Salt Lake City, UT 84150
801–240–1201
www.lds.org

Laubach Literacy Action (large literacy organization with world programs)
1320 Jamesville Ave., Box 131
Syracuse, NY 13210
888–LAUBACH (528–2224)
www.laubach.org/International/indexinternational.html

Lutheran World Relief
700 Light St.
Baltimore, MD 21230
410–230–2800
www.lwr.org

Mercy Corps International
3015 SW First Ave.
Portland, OR 97201
800–292–3355, ext. 250
www.mercycorps.org

Operation Smile (international medical missions, student programs)
6435 Tidewater Dr.
Norfolk, VA 23509
757–321–7645
www.operationsmile.org

Oxfam America (student programs, volunteering)
26 West St.
Boston, MA 02111–1206
800–77–OXFAM
www.oxfamamerica.org

Oxfam International
266 Banbury Rd., Suite 20
Oxford OX2 7D2
England
44 1865 31 39 39
www.oxfam.org

Peace Corps
1111 20th St., NW
Washington D.C. 20526
800–424–8580
www.peacecorps.gov

Project Concern International (health program that uses volunteers and
    students)
3550 Afton Rd.
San Diego, CA 92123
858–279–9690
www.projectconcern.org

Rotary International: A Global Network of Community Volunteers
One Rotary Center
1560 Sherman Ave.
Evanston, IL 60201
847–866–3000
www.rotary.org

SAPE (formerly "The Soviet-American Penfriend Exchange," SAPE is
looking for more than 100,000 "snail mail" American pen pals to
write letters to people in the Baltics and former Soviet Union)
P. O. Box 319
Monroe, CT 06468–0319
www.michander.com/sape/menu-e.html

Sister Cities International (sustainable, long-term partnerships in cities
all over the world, as well as short-term partnerships for specific sub-
stantive projects)
1301 Pennsylvania Ave., NW
Suite 850
Washington D.C. 20004
202–347–8630
www.sister-cities.org

Soroptimist of the Americas (a volunteer service organization for
women)
Two Penn Center Plaza
Suite 1000
Philadelphia, PA 19102–1883
215–557–9300
www.soroptimist.org/

World Learning
Kipling Rd., P. O. Box 676
Brattleboro, VT 05302–0676
802–257–7751
www.worldlearning.org

# LEGAL

*Ius est ars boni et aequi (Legal justice is the art of the good and the fair).*
—Latin Saying

Many people without money for legal services don't know that free advice is available. State legal-aid organizations are trying to change that. Attorneys with skill and compassion are the most likely volunteers, giving of their time to help others with legal problems and assist the staff of legal-aid

- ● Groups
- ♥ Families
- ★ Youth
- ♥ Professional Qualifications
- ໃ Training Required

services. Other volunteers may help serve the half million children under government supervision; everyone can make a difference in this capacity by:

*Recognizing the need for making legal services available to all people.*

*Directing indigent immigrants, the elderly, people with disabilities and low or no income to available legal services. Good legal advice can prevent problems.*

*Being aware of the needs of children in state custody.*

## WHAT IS CASA?

Court Appointed Special Advocates (CASA) are ordinary citizen volunteers appointed by the court to represent children in state care. There are currently 710 CASA programs in all fifty states and the District of Columbia. By using volunteers, the community participates with the social and justice systems to find the best possible solutions for children who have been removed from their homes because of abuse, neglect, or abandonment. "Justice for all" depends on a lot of people who are willing to help. CASA volunteers do not need to have a legal background but are screened closely (including a background check) for objectivity, competence, and commitment.

To be a CASA volunteer, you will need twenty-four hours of initial training and twelve hours of inservice training each year thereafter. A volunteer commits at least twelve hours a month. CASA volunteers might do one or all of the following:

- Spend time with a child one-on-one both in the current home environment and away. ☙
- Serve as a fact-finder for the judge by thoroughly researching the background of each child assigned. ☙
- Work with the child's attorney (Guardian ad Litem) to figure out what is best for the child. ☙
- Speak for the child in the courtroom, representing his or her best interests. ☙
- Continue to act as a "watchdog" for the child during the life of the case, ensuring that it is brought to a swift and appropriate conclusion. ☙

When a judge appoints a volunteer to a child's case, the volunteer becomes an officer of the court to speak exclusively for the child's best interest. To prepare, the volunteer should talk with the child, family members, neighbors, school officials, therapists, doctors—anyone who is involved in the child's life; review all records and documents involved in the case; submit a formal report recommending placement.

Decisions are then made determining whether the child should stay with his or her parents, stay in an out-of-home placement/foster care situation, or be freed for permanent adoption. Volunteers are assigned to only one or two cases at a time, whereas agency

> *Every attorney is a member of the third branch of government, the judicial branch, whether or not they go to court. And every attorney has an obligation to bring the benefits of that branch of government, the rule of law, to people.*
>
> *—David O. Nuffer, Federal Court Magistrate*

staff members average sixty to ninety cases at any given time. Child advocacy is significant service.

## VOLUNTEER LEGAL SERVICES

People do not have to be attorneys to facilitate the flow of legal services to the needy. Basic training is given to people with a desire to assist. College students, law students, and even high school students can help and gain valuable experience at the same time. Paralegals, legal secretaries, court recorders, and people with clerical skills are instantly useful. Assistance is needed in legal service organizations that supply advice and representation. Volunteers can:

> *It was on a Sunday morning, my son and I were leaving for church. My husband awoke and he was just in complete rage. . . .*
>
> *Through Legal Aid we were able to have this protection order. . . . They really provided a format for me and a process that enabled me to take each step one at a time and move from leaving my home into a more secure independent emotional situation.*
>
> *—Kathleen, client of Legal Aid Services*

- Perform initial client interviews over the phone (using scripts). ⚔
- Help older citizens seeking protection from physical abuse and financial exploitation. ♥ ⚔
- Draft documents, type letters. ★ ♥ ⚔
- Research social service agencies and other referral sources; maintain referral files. ★
- Assist training coordinators with preparation and presentation of materials. ★
- Translate for clients.

## VOLUNTEER ATTORNEYS

Attorneys are experts in an area that intimidates most others. A practicing lawyer has sufficient background to help provide the typically needed legal services. Volunteer attorneys are the backbone of pro bono clinics and the resource for cases requiring

*There is good news and bad news. The good news is that the volunteer attorneys who do pro bono work do it out of the goodness of their hearts. They are compassionate and positive; they look forward to helping and they feel the rewards. I consider them my best friends. The bad news is there are only a handful.*

—*Patrick Pan, pro bono director, Utah Legal Services*

representation. Legal-aid organizations try to smooth the attorney's role with support from law students, updates on relevant areas of the law, and malpractice coverage. Volunteer attorneys are needed to help with many services that do not involve ongoing representation. Two-hour shifts once a month may include:

- *Pro se* clinics (coaching clients representing themselves on court procedures)
- A hearing (one-time advice and representation of low-income tenants trying to avoid eviction)
- Street clinics (resolving a variety of legal and social issues with clients in poverty-serving agencies, including assistance to victims of abuse in women's shelters)
- Estate planning (preparation of wills or trusts, deeds, powers of attorney, and advance medical directives. Volunteer attorneys may meet with clients in nursing homes, hospitals, and private homes, as well as in the office.)
- Initial intake interviews
- Night courts (which lighten the case load for judges and help a large number of people quickly)
- Training sessions for:

  Rules of evidence

  Trial tactics

  Witness examination techniques

  Advanced practice tips in areas of

  Landlord-tenant relations

  Subsidized housing

  Disability

Estate planning

Domestic relations

American Indian law

Medicaid/Medicare/health programs

After all the screening and advising is done, there are still many people who need legal services that they can't pay for. There are busy times when staff can't cover all the hearings throughout the state. Qualified attorneys can:

- Agree to be on the legal-aid referral list.

- Represent people in civil cases.

- Assist social services agencies when they are over-loaded by attending a hearing in a part of the state where you live or work, for example.

## Internet Resources

CASAnet (support web site for CASA)
www. casanet.org

The Equal Justice Network (information for people giving civil legal
    assistance to the low-income population)
www.equaljustice.org

## Organizations

Contact local offices of the Guardian Ad Litem and CASA through your state's legal services division.

The National Court-Appointed Special Advocate Association
100 W. Harrison St., Suite 500
North Tower
Seattle, WA 98119
800–628–3233
www.nationalcasa.org

National Legal Aid & Defender Association
1625 K St., NW, Suite 800
Washington D.C. 20006–1604
202–452–0620
www.nlada.org

# MENTAL

*The imposition of stigma is the commonest form of violence used in democratic societies.*

—R. A. Pinker

At least one in ten families has experienced the pain and struggle associated with caring for a mentally ill loved one. One of the toughest aspects of caring for someone with a mental illness is the lack of understanding from the people families must come in contact with from day to day. People generally do not cause their own mental afflictions. Unfortunately, society today tends to be plagued with the same blaming syndrome documented centuries ago: "Who did sin, this man, or his parents, that he was born blind?" Now, like then, the answer is most often "neither." But everyone can begin to have more empathy, and thus make a difference to those afflicted with this disease, by:

- ● Groups
- ♥ Families
- ★ Youth
- ♥ Professional Qualifications
- ☧ Training Required

> *Treating people with mental illnesses, permanent mental disorders, and common forms of learning disabilities with understanding, patience, and respect.*
>
> *Slowing down enough to understand how someone with a mental disorder functions best.*

## MENTAL ILLNESS

Mental illness may be better described as a correctable chemical imbalance. One in five people, in fact, suffers some mild form of mental illness in any given year for relatively brief periods of time (National Institute of Mental Health Executive Summary, Bethesda, MD). However, for the five million adults with severe mental illnesses, their pain is exacerbated by society's misunderstanding, fear, and stigmatization. Some of the most gifted and giving people in society struggle with mental illness and deserve our help.

> As for me, you must know I shouldn't precisely have chosen madness if there had been any choice. What consoles me is that I am beginning to consider madness as an illness like any other, and that I accept it as such.
>
> —Vincent Van Gogh

Mental disorders are a group of individual illnesses of the brain that affect behavior, mood, and even thinking processes. Most people with a mental illness can recover. Furthermore, treatment is prevention. People who receive the right medication on a regular basis can usually avoid psychotic episodes. Left untreated, mental and emotional disorders may lead to substance abuse, suicide, or prison. To help, you can:

*Encourage proper diagnosis.*

*Support appropriate treatment.*

When someone dearly loved has a mental illness that turns normal life upside down, family members may be the best ones to help. Those afflicted with schizophrenia, bipolar disorder (manic depression), clinical depression, panic disorders, and obsessive-compulsive disorder need assistance from people close at hand. Both the suffering individual and the family may gain experience that uniquely qualifies them to become effective trainers who serve others by:

- Participating in family-to-family education. One family may be trained to teach a course to others, supplemented with a lot of personal experience. ♥ ⚧

- Participating in consumer-to-consumer education offered free by and to people who are recovering from mental illness. People with personal experience can most effectively share not only facts but feelings. ⚧

> *I have bipolar disorder. I received my BS, MS, and CAGS, and also did some doctoral studies, which I had to give up pursuing due to my illness.*
>
> *Even with medication and therapy I had a series of twenty hospitalizations over a sixteen-year period. . . . I still experience rapid cycling.*
>
> *I've discovered the key leading to recovery is proper consistent medical supervision and treatment, support of family and friends, and accepting responsibility for doing all you can to help yourself.*
>
> *I am aware that I will probably never be able to return to gainful employment, but I can use my skills and knowledge to benefit others.*
>
> —Shiela Monahan, volunteer in a special education high school program

Mental illness is increasing. Thirteen percent of American children suffer from mental disorders and 70 percent of those do not receive treatment ("Hope For Tomorrow: Mental Health Education Program For Schools," brochure, NAMI Utah). More and more college students are lining up at counseling centers for intensive therapy or medication or both (see Rachel Hartigan Shea, "On the Edge on Campus: The State of College Students' Mental Health Continues to Decline," *U.S. News and World Report*, 18 February 2002). No group of society is immune, but all major risk factors are more prevalent at lower socioeconomic levels (National Institute of Mental Health, Executive Summary). Volunteers are needed to conduct mental health education programs in schools and may be asked to:

- Teach about brain chemistry and mood and thought disorders. ✗
- Teach about the physical and mental effects of eating disorders. ✗
- Teach about addictive disorders, such as alcohol and substance abuse. ✗

Alcohol and other drugs can cause or increase mental illness and are major causes of the epidemic in homeless and prison populations. Government, as well as private nonprofit organizations, support many programs for the mentally ill, including day treatment and live-in rehabilitation centers. Staff is always on hand to assist in crisis situations. Many centers need volunteers to:

- Tutor

- Teach rehabilitation and employment skills (such as wellness, cooking, computer education, and so on) ●

- Assist with clerical duties

- Simply hang out

The mentally ill may suffer from delusions and hallucinations, which are common among stroke, Alzheimer, schizophrenic, and some bi-polar patients during the manic phase. In your work with them, communication is essential for calming them down. You should also be aware of how to de-escalate psychotic episodes. First, be ready to strike up a conversation about anything at hand (a poster, what's on the TV). This will usually distract the person. Also try to keep the person talking and be sincere. People can tell if you are really concerned about their welfare—and only then will they respond.

> *Our son Mark was diagnosed with schizophrenia when he was 16 years old. It took more than two years before doctors and therapists found a treatment regimen that really healed him. The roller coaster of emotions that our family suffered was devastating.*
>
> *Mark is at a point now where he has a job, he has feelings of value and self-worth. Our relationship with him is very satisfying—recovery is possible.*
>
> *I can now spend the time serving that I used to spend in crisis.*
>
> *—Dic and Jennifer, parent advocates for the mentally ill*

## PEOPLE WITH PERVASIVE DEVELOPMENTAL DISORDERS (PDDs)

PDDs include a whole spectrum of disorders most commonly associated with the term *autism*. Disorders such as autism may have a strong genetic component but, like a mental illness, may also prove to be somewhat treatable. People with autism and similar disorders may look normal and can often be misjudged as undisciplined and lacking in common sense. But they also may have good mental capacity that, if properly channeled, can accomplish much. Behavior training is critical for all developmental disorders. There is a lot that families and people in general can do to assist:

- Simply learn about the characteristics of the disorder; this will increase empathy and awareness. ● ♥ ★

- Teach the person language skills and social skills. ⚎

- Offer respite care to the parents. ● ♥ ★

Increasing awareness of autism is generating more autism centers and local societies throughout the United States. These centers need volunteers to assist with:

- Parent-to-parent befriending

- Answering questions over the phone

- Categorizing educational materials and creating a resource library

- Assisting with conferences, family meetings, and parents' nights out ★

- Center improvement projects: construction of picnic tables, art easels, corner chairs, and stepping blocks (good Eagle Scout projects), book donations, and so on ● ★

- Group activities in places with special schools and/or pre-schools ● ★

---

*Our best volunteer is a former client. He was referred here from the shelter after having lost his wife to cancer. We helped him get housing and he's been coming back ever since. He stays at the food and coffee corner, crass and crude and as good as they get. He knows how to dish it out—sets limits, tells people to cool off or take a walk. . . . Everybody tells him everything, he knows more than the caseworkers. We take turns driving him home to catch up on the scoop.*

*—Staff member from Safe Haven, a homeless facility for the mentally ill*

## BUILDING ABILITIES IN PEOPLE WHO ARE MENTALLY CHALLENGED

Mental retardation is an unexplained mystery in 75 percent of cases and is usually a lifelong condition (see "Medical Encyclopedia," at http://health.aol.drkoop.com/conditions/ency/article.asp?id=1523). Only 5 percent of people with mental retardation are profoundly impaired. The rest, depending on the amount of socialization and intervention, may lead fairly normal lives. Adults with mental retardation are not "children." They may remain remarkably childlike but they want to be treated with respect, not condescension. Loving an artless, guileless person is easy for some but requires considerable patience and adjustment for many others.

Being mentally challenged no longer precludes an individual from jobs, schooling, independent living, and participation in sports. Early diagnosis facilitates special training from infancy. Children who are expected to read, to write, to sing, to swim, to dance, and to play ball—probably will. As you work with mentally retarded children, you will find that their personalities are as varied as the general populace, and they are usually happier and more involved as part of a family. Here are some general rules for your volunteer interaction:

> We like having a group home (for the mentally challenged) across the street. They bring us cookies and we take some back. They call us "sister" and "mom." The one named Linda always asks if she can have a soda pop so we keep plenty in the refrigerator but she never stays long; her attention span is very short. Linda loves the pesky dog next door to lick her face.
>
> Those women make the neighborhood a lot more fun. They'll lay out in the summer time in long pants. The store managers all know them—talk to them and let them use the bathroom. They have jobs; we see them catching the bus every day. One stole a piece of candy from Top Stop; the police came but didn't know what to do. She was standing there just sobbing her heart out. They're cute—just like little kids.
>
> —Ashley Thomas, college student

*Be friendly; acknowledge the individual by name, engage in conversation.*

*Include the person in all kinds of activities; participation enlarges abilities and social skills.*

*Invite them to help you; tutor them; they can learn a wide range of job skills and be excellent workers.*

*Don't hide a sensitive or heady discussion from them; they do not have to understand what is being said to feel your acceptance.*

*Look for body language to reveal moods and reactions; their faces and words may not reflect their true feelings (they may say "yes" to every question just to please you).*

*Accept extreme reactions to sadness or disappointment (tearful outburst, hiding face, leaving abruptly).*

*Don't underestimate their capacities: a forty-year-old with the mental capacity of a seven-year-old has thirty-three years more experience.*

*Supply extra reassurance during times of stress; changes may require more time for adjustment.*

*Be patient with retelling.*

- Contact a local Arc (Advocates for the Rights of Citizens with Mental Retardation) chapter

- Volunteer to befriend a person with a disability who has no support system; let her talk, go for walks, invite him out for ice cream, give a birthday present. ● ♥ ★

- Volunteer to care for a mentally disabled child while his or her parents have a night out. ♥ ★

- Volunteer to be an advocate; ensure that the person with developmental disabilities is getting the necessary services (contact local ARC office).

- Volunteer with your area's Special Olympics program. Special Olympics provides year-round sports training and athletic competition in a variety of summer and winter sports for people with mental retardation aged eight and up. The benefits are mental, social, and spiritual—they develop skills along with boundless courage and enthusiasm. For those with profound disabilities there are programs that emphasize training rather than competition. Participation is free and depends on volunteers (individuals or families). At the Special Olympics, you can:

Be a coach. ★

Volunteer at events.

Train athletes at home (between practices).

Provide transportation to practices and competitions.

Be a chaperone.

Attend competitions as spectators. ● ♥ ★

> *The biggest thrill I've had was during the district Special Olympics swimming last year. At the beginning of the games I was asked to have a student carry in the Olympic torch. She has comelia delange syndrome—small squatty body with a bit of a hump—but I helped her hold it up high (it was really burning) and we walked the whole way to the stand and then on back to our place to great applause from everyone. Her mother was in tears saying how she would always remember the time that Amanda was the star!*
>
> *—Midge Edwards, special education teacher*

## Organizations

Goodwill Industries (www.goodwill.org) and Deseret Industries (801–240–3642) have training programs to help people with mental disabilities gain employment. Their programs depend on in-kind donations.

The Department of Veterans Affairs (www.va.gov/volunteer) has local volunteer opportunities serving people with mental disorders.

American Health Care Association
1201 L St., NW
Washington D.C. 20005
202–842–4444
www.ahca.org (click on Sites of Interest, Developmentally Disabled sites
    and Intermediate Care Facilities for the Mentally Retarded)

The Arc (the national organization of and for people with mental retar-
    dation and related developmental disabilities)
1010 Wayne Ave., Suite 650
Silver Springs, Maryland 20910
301–565–3842
www.thearc.org

Autism Society of America
7910 Woodmont Ave., Suite 650
Bethesda, MD 20814
301–657–0881
www.autism-society.org

Bazelon Center for Mental Health Law
1101 15th St., NW, Suite 1212
Washington D.C. 20005–5002
202–467-5730
www.bazelon.org

International Center for Clubhouse Development (varied names locally
    i.e. Alliance House)
425 W. 47th St.
New York City, NY 10036
212–582–0343
www.iccd.org (click on clubhouse directory, international)

NAMI: National Alliance for the Mentally Ill
Colonial Place Three
2107 Wilson Blvd.
Suite 300
Arlington, VA 22201–3042
703–524–7600  Helpline: 800–950–NAMI
www.nami.org

National Ability Center (one of several training centers for Paralympic
    and Special Olympic participants)
P. O. Box 682799
Quinn's Junction, Highways 248 & 40
Park City, UT 84068
435–649–3991
www.nationalabilitycenter.org

National Down Syndrome Society (NDSS)
666 Broadway
New York, NY 10012
800–221–4602
www.ndss.org

Special Olympics
1325 G St., NW, Suite 500
Washington D.C. 20005
202–628–3630
www.specialolympics.org

Splore (one of many expedition/camp programs for people with develop-
    mental/other disabilities)
880 E. 3375 S.
Salt Lake City, UT 84106
801–484–4128
www.splore@splore.org

Sprout (a non-profit committed to travel and recreation for people with
    special needs)
893 Amsterdam Ave.
New York, NY 10025
212–222–9575
http://users.rcn.com/sprout.interport

# OFFICE AND ADMINISTRATIVE WORK

*Helping is the true vocation of every human being, and we don't have to wait
for some terrible event to come and reveal it to us.*

—*Eknath Easwaran*

The decision to volunteer in an office is a decision to join a team effort toward a goal. Offices are hubs of activity where interaction with other people moves a cause along. The variety of possible activities is endless. But the choice of

- ● Groups
- ♥ Families
- ★ Youth
- ♥ Professional Qualifications
- ♀ Training Required

causes is individual. Choose your cause first, then make sure you're working with the right people. Nearly every agency, organization, school, and hospital needs help with office work. Starting in an office may give you a sense for the whole organization if it's fairly small; large organizations may vary greatly between departments. General rules to observe so that you can make a difference include:

*Recognize that there may be a healthy but uneasy comradery
between paid and volunteer help, even though paid staff tend
to do better work alongside volunteers and volunteers can
learn a lot from paid staff.*

*Slip into a position and lift gently; don't rock the ship.*

*Remember that service is contagious. Good volunteers can*
*inspire paid staff to volunteer somewhere else.*

## HELP NEEDED IN AN OFFICE

Most service agencies need help to:

- Answer phones; direct visitors.
- Take messages; make reminder calls.
- Answer crisis hot-lines during non business hours. ✗
- Compile mailings, label/address envelopes. ● ★
- Give information over the phone; make referrals. ✗
- Record and transcribe minutes of meetings.
- Collect/enter data.
- File, index, copy, schedule.
- Distribute mail; act as a courier. ★
- Screen records/do intake.
- Assemble orientation packets (may be done at home). ● ★
- Distribute flyers. ● ★
- Do graphic design, photography, scrap booking.
- Guide tours. ✗
- Design and manage a Web site. ✗
- Sort/record donations.
- Staff an information booth. ● ★

## HELP NEEDED IN ADMINISTRATION

The objectives of volunteers and paid staff should be identical. Both want the organization to succeed and improve the lives of others. Volunteers may be just as well trained as paid staff but prefer the flexibility of not being employed. Other qualified volunteers don't need the money but are simply happy to help out. Many administrative opportunities are available. Volunteers can:

- Serve as office manager/administrative assistant. ☧
- Organize services and activities in the community. ●
- Organize fund-raising events. ●
- Educate the public on available classes/services.
- Create appealing exhibits. ● ★
- Become a board member/attend meetings.
- Consult on vocational projects. ♥
- Represent a foundation at community events.
- Teach computer and literacy courses. ☧
- Organize and develop volunteer opportunities.
- Create a skills-development program (one-on-one). ♥ ☧
- Assist with leadership training.

## WRITING

All writers should utilize basic rules: be brief, be clear, and be a storyteller. Remember that specific illustrations grab and hold attention. Organizations are always interested in a volunteer who is willing to write articles for bulletins, newspapers, or magazines. You might volunteer to:

> *Easy work is as rewarding as steering a parked car.*
>
> —Max De Pree, *author of* Leading without Power: Finding Hope in Serving Community

- Write press releases about the organization's efforts and work.
- Publish company newsletters.
- Copyedit or proofread materials for publication.
- Help administrators write Letters of information/recommendation.

Many nonprofit organizations don't have the time or resources to write interesting articles about their own progress. So a volunteer who writes for them is particularly valuable. Before accepting a writing assignment, obtain a clear understanding of the material to be covered, know expected length of the finished product, and ask about the anticipated deadline for review and completion. Learn whether you will be expected to do interviews, develop the material yourself, or be supplied information to write up and format.

## COMPUTERS

Office work is no longer limited to the office. The options of virtual volunteering from home or work—wherever one has Internet access—is growing. It allows people with time constraints, home-based obligations, and disabilities to contribute. Some volunteering by computer can be done on flexible schedules; other opportunities require specific committed hours of availability. Questions that might help you know if you are suited to virtual volunteering include:

> *I like things down in black and white. I like reports, documents, data entry, and schedules. Straightening things out on the volunteer board suits me just fine. And people appreciate it. I've had members of the board say things like, "Thanks, we like that new manual," "We needed the by-laws updated," "The handbook is easier to use." I'm an organizer. I definitely get a feeling of accomplishment.*
>
> *—Jim Biddiscombe, volunteer services, Shriners Hospital*

- Do you have regular, ongoing access to the Internet?

- Are you a good writer?

- Do you have a set time of day when you can work on virtual assignments?

- Do you answer your E-mail messages promptly?

- Will you have freedom to work on volunteer assignments without distractions?

If you answered affirmatively, then you would be well suited for virtual volunteering. Almost anything you can do on a computer to help out can be considered a volunteer opportunity. For example, you could:

- Provide free legal advice. ♥
- Type a term paper for a person with a disability. ★
- Stay in contact with a shut-in who has E-mail. ★
- Write conference reviews/talk summaries.
- Provide graphic design. ♥ ⚷
- Do simple accounting. ♥ ⚷
- Translate materials.

For more information on volunteering in this capacity, contact a Volunteer Center for a list of administrative/office service opportunities.

## Internet Resources

www.serviceleader.org (lists virtual volunteering needs)

www.volunteerconnections.org (Volunteer Center National Network)

www.volunteermatch.org (lists volunteer opportunities by area)

www.volunteermatch.org/virtual/ (lists virtual volunteering opportunities)

# REFUGEES AND IMMIGRANTS

*Give me your tired, your poor, huddled masses yearning to breathe free, the wretched refuse of your teeming shore. Send these, the homeless, tempest-tossed to me.*

—*From the base of the Statue of Liberty*

Countries are prohibited under international law from returning refugees to persecution, but they are not required to take them in. The idea of asylum is part of ancient Arabic and Israelite traditions. The early history of America also includes many refugees—those fleeing religious persecution.

- ● **Groups**
- ♥ **Families**
- ★ **Youth**
- ♥ **Professional Qualifications**
- ⚐ **Training Required**

Everyone can make a difference in the life of an immigrant or refugee by:

*Viewing refugees as survivors, not victims*

*Encouraging independence and self-reliance right from the start*

*Being a friend; help refugees and immigrants to feel part of their new American culture.*

## HELPING TO RESETTLE

Through the years, America has given refuge to millions. When a person seeks refuge here, protection and assistance organizations first encourage the refugee to return home voluntarily if and when the situation becomes safe. Refugees are then encouraged to integrate into the country of their first asylum. As a last resort, refugees are assisted in resettling in a third country. Despite this policy, 14 million refugees remain currently displaced (*World Refugee Survey 2000*, U.S. Committee for Refugees, 2002). Most refugees to the United States come here from several parts of Africa, Eastern Europe, and the Near East. The United States government provides a no-interest loan, some starter assistance of food stamps, a Social Security card, and eight months Refugee Cash Assistance. The government assures refugee assistance in several other areas, usually supplied by charitable organizations with much help from volunteers and generous citizens. Refugee organizations in the United States need a lot of help. Caseworkers have large loads and depend entirely on donations for start-up supplies and help in many other ways (depending on the local office). If you volunteer to help with a refugee assistance program, you might provide:

> *There is always a touch of irony when a citizen of the United States complains about immigration. Except for those of pure Native American origin, every one of us is of immigrant descent. With each new influx of immigrants, the older population has balked. Chances are, what is said today about Hispanic immigrants was once said about your own ancestors.*
>
> —*Brian Frazelle, volunteer at a house of hospitality for Latin American immigrants*

- Housing assistance, furnishings (including furniture, kitchen utensils, bedding), food, and clothing ● ♥
- Airport greetings
- Mentoring of a refugee one-on-one for four to six months
- ESL tutoring
- Computer tutoring
- Technical tutoring, such as teaching job skills ♥
- Transportation assistance
- Bilingual reception work
- Interpretations for medical appointments

- Adopt-a-family service for the holidays ♥ ● ★

- Pro bono counseling; assisting with post-traumatic stress disorder ♥

The guiding principle in refugee settlement agencies is to help people enough at the front end so they can regain control of their lives and start helping others who come after them. But there are specific guidelines, and organizations warn against the "renegade" volunteer—one who gives far more than suggested to one family, leaving other families jealous and discontented.

> *People ask me why I arrange for volunteers to adopt a family of refugees during the Christian holidays when many of these people are Muslim. I tell them that refugees need all the help they can get, and since people feel more like giving at Christmastime of course we encourage it—just be sensitive about when Ramadan falls and avoid beef. These families use everything they are given. After the basics, the top requested item on most wish lists is a vacuum.*
>
> —Beth Bedbury, Volunteer Coordinator, Catholic Community Services

## HELPING IMMIGRANTS

Immigrants may be on their own from the start; the federal government is not committed to assistance. Yet, immigrants are the ones who have worked and dreamed their way here, desiring above all else to make America their home. Several nonprofit organizations have developed programs to give immigrants a place to gather and receive advice. Immigrant services are looking for volunteers to help do the following:

- Teach English.

- Provide childcare while parents learn. ● ♥ ★

- Assist immigrants with completing forms.

- Interpret and translate.

- Assist with resume preparation.

- Provide immigrants with information on social services, schools, health care, housing, recreational facilities. ⚹

People can also help through organizations that serve in immigrant neighborhoods by:

- Offering community education classes ♥
- Providing legal services ♥

## More Ideas for Expanding Service

Some charitable organizations don't discriminate between refugees and poor immigrants. They depend on volunteers to help them support both. These organizations do some of the following:

- Situate refugees and immigrants in accessible neighborhoods.
- Provide volunteer opportunities for refugees and immigrants.
- Teach them leadership and organizational skills as volunteers.
- Provide them a place to create their own cultural organizations.
- Allow them to grow strong enough as a group to start helping refugees and immigrants from other cultures.

*I have always wanted to live in America. My parents tried to have me in the U.S. but I was born just across the border. After I graduated from school I came here on a visitor visa. It took many years to get a work permit but I knew it would happen. Now I assist a kindergarten teacher with many Hispanic children in her class. I can improve my English. I love America. I will be a citizen some day and my children will be born here—like in my dreams.*

*—Betsabé Martinez López, student teacher*

## Suggested Reading

Mary Pipher, *The Middle of Everywhere: The World's Refugees Come to Our Town*, New York: Harcourt, 2002.

## Internet Resources

U. S. Committee for Refugees (USCR)
www.refugees.org

## Organizations

Contact local multi-cultural centers (community recreation centers), local YWCA, local Catholic Social Services, and local literacy centers, all of which assist refugees and use volunteers.

American Friends Service Committee (provides information and services to immigrants with the help of volunteers)
1501 Cherry St.
Philadelphia, PA 19102
215–241–7000
www.afsc.org

Church World Service (updates on world refugees)
Resource Development and Service Center
28606 Phillips St., P. O. Box 968
Elkhart, IN 46515
800–297–1516
www.churchworldservice.org

International Rescue Committee (assists with resettlement; directory of local offices)
122 E. 42nd St., 12th Floor
New York City, NY 10168–1289
212–551–3000
www.intrescom.org

Literacy Volunteers of America
1330 Jamesville Ave.
Syracuse, NY 13210
315–472–0001
www.literacyvolunteers.org

# RELIGION

*The world cannot always understand one's profession of faith, but it can understand service.*

*—Ian Maclaren*

Religion is deeply personal and prompts an inward journey of discovery—a discovery of self and of our relationship with God. The outcome is never self-absorbed, for the realm of the spiritual prompts participation. Those who find pure religion discover within themselves energy to serve others.

● Groups
♥ Families
★ Youth
♥ Professional Qualifications
ʃ Training Required

According to Harvard professor and scholar Robert Putnam, nearly half of all associations in America are church related, half of all personal philanthropy is religious in nature, and half of all volunteering occurs in a religious context (*Bowling Alone: The Collapse and Revival of American Community* [New York: Simon & Schuster, 2000], 66). Religious organizations form the backbone of service in America. Even if you don't volunteer on a regular basis with an organized religious group, you can still practice a few general principles that will generate a feeling of charity:

> *Nurture spiritual habits. Meditate (people who reflect on truth, who recognize goodness, and who appreciate beauty are resilient), study religious texts (people who learn from scriptural examples save themselves from harsh experience and*

*maintain courage), and pray (people who pray define life's important questions and prepare themselves for answers).*

*Grow in wisdom; evaluate results of service and make adjustments to constantly improve.*

*Resist giving "gilded lily" service in one's own congregation while failing to see the needs of others on the outside.*

## CHURCH SERVICE

People who worship in the same church are quick to help each other. Churches depend on the willing support of their members. There are plenty of volunteer opportunities right within your own congregation:

- Assist with formal worship services.
- Staff nurseries. ★
- Sing in choirs. ★
- Teach Sunday school classes.
- Lead youth organizations.
- Lead Scout troops.
- Organize sports programs.
- Participate in charitable service groups.
- Plan church socials.

Participation in all of these functions helps individuals to develop the qualities of character in which members believe, strengthens families, and perpetuates vitality in the community. At times when participation in these activities seems like

> *As with physical exercise, those of us who say we haven't the time for "spiritual aerobics" are excuse making and will find ourselves, whenever the situation calls for strength beyond our reserve, incapacitated by self-doubt, envy, jealousy, pride, fear, anger, bad tempers, all indicating a lack of spiritual oxygen.*
>
> *We must never become too busy sawing to take time to sharpen the saw.*
>
> —*Stephen R. Covey, author of* Seven Habits of Highly Effective People

more than enough, individuals can sift, balance, and prioritize. The purpose of church activity is always to nourish the desire to serve, never to burn it out.

## Reaching Out

People who serve in religious organizations are also the ones who tend to reach out and befriend, and even recruit, people in the community to support other worthy projects (see Putnam, *Bowling Alone*, 66). Extending time and talents from within a congregation to the broader community can be as important a form of service. Church members may:

> *For the past two years I have served in a care center for intellectually impaired adults. I have learned priceless lessons from them—lessons of humility, love, kindness, patience. . . . I've learned to value our differences, for they spawn opportunities for service.*
>
> *—Mark G. Warner, ecclesiastical leader of worship services held in a care center for intellectually impaired adults*

- Take worship services and activity programs into care centers, hospitals, housing units for the elderly and people with disabilities. ♥ ★

- Send members to regularly visit people in nearby health care institutions. ♥ ★

- Help the elderly and those with disabilities living in nearby apartment buildings to shop or do laundry. ♥ ★

- Host the homeless through interfaith hospitality networks.

- Do a service project with a youth group: help clean yards, rake leaves, shovel snow; make newborn or birth mother kits for donation; start an adopt a highway or adopt a grandparent program. ★

- Serve any kind of mission.

Churches are often uniquely helpful in times of emergency— during floods, hurricanes, brush fires, tornadoes, and so on.

Members may already have an established organization in which members can volunteer to do one or more of the following:

- Account for people in the neighborhood.
- Assist with evacuations.
- Provide housing for families in need. ♥
- Set up a command post and temporary eating and sleeping facilities in a meetinghouse.
- Lead efforts to clean up and rebuild.

> *Firefighters predicted the Mauers would lose their home. Instead, for 14 days church members helped fight the fires, cleared bushland, watched children, shifted furniture, hauled water and cooked meals for the Mauers and other church and community members.*
>
> *Brothers and sisters worked shoulder to shoulder with rural bush fire brigades to protect homes. Of the many properties that were under threat only one shed was lost.*
>
> —*Sarah Jane Weaver, newswriter*

## JOINT SPONSORSHIP

Congregations may build considerable goodwill by joining together to sponsor joint activities that unite and empower the whole community. Inclusion is a powerful spiritual principle. Creating settings that uplift and unify people of different backgrounds, occupations, and social groups helps to build a broader community ethic. People serve by joining in support of:

- Thanksgiving worship services, Independence Day patriotic services, and other holiday gatherings ♥ ★
- Anti-crime programs
- Faith-based counseling
- Community education and literacy programs
- Cultural festivals for local holidays
- Strengthening-the-family workshops
- Drug and substance abuse programs

## Principles in Action

People of faith serve with a bright hope and an unconditional love for others. Spiritually based service organizations are unique in that they may choose to include religious concepts and language in their programs. Much of their effectiveness lies in infusing value-based programs with spiritual vitality and adherence to well-defined principles. The power of true principles is in evidence through the more than one hundred other programs that have adopted and adapted the Twelve Steps of Alcoholics Anonymous.

> *Forgiveness is not easy.*
>
> *It is still difficult in the privacy of the bedroom to say, "Sorry." Yet it is a powerful source of new beginnings. It means, "OK, I give you another chance to make a fresh start."*
>
> *In our country, if we had not decided to forgive each other, it would have gone up in flames. Tit for tat, an eye for an eye, doesn't give stability or security.*
>
> —Desmond Tutu

1. We admitted we were powerless over alcohol—that our lives had become unmanageable.

2. We came to believe that a Power greater than ourselves could restore us to sanity.

3. We made a decision to turn our will and our lives over to the care of God *as we understood Him.*

4. We made a searching and fearless moral inventory of ourselves.

5. We admitted to God, to ourselves, and to another human being the exact nature of our wrongs.

6. We were entirely ready to have God remove all these defects of character.

7. We humbly asked Him to remove our shortcomings.

8. We made a list of all persons we had harmed, and became willing to make amends to them all.

9. We made direct amends to such people wherever possible, except when to do so would injure them or others.

10. We continued to take personal inventory, and when we were wrong promptly admitted it.

11. We sought through prayer and meditation to improve our conscious contact with God *as we understood Him,* praying only for knowledge of His will for us and the power to carry that out.

12. Having had a spiritual awakening as the result of these steps, we tried to carry this message to alcoholics and to practice these principles in all our affairs.

Practicing these steps in our homes, communities, and the world will surely make a difference regardless of our organized volunteer efforts; and that difference may just be the best form of service we can provide.

## Internet Resources

Families Worldwide (a resource for strengthening relationships in the
   home)
www.fww.org

## Organizations

Most church social service programs are found through local churches; contact them for ways in which to help. Other religious based social services that are best assisted locally are Habitat for Humanity (www.habitat.org), The Salvation Army (www.salvationarmy.org), Volunteers of America (www.voa.org), YMCA (www.ymca.net), and YWCA (www.ywca.org)

National religion based service organizations that help without regard to religious affiliation, ethnicity, or nationality include:

Catholic Network of Volunteer Service (connects full-time volunteers
   with Christian member programs)
1410 Q St., NW
Washington D.C. 20009
800–543–5046
www.cnvs.org

Humanitarian Services of The Church of Jesus Christ of Latter-day
    Saints
50 E. North Temple, Floor 7
Salt Lake City, UT 84150
801–240–1201
www.lds.org

Lutheran Services in America
700 Light St.
Baltimore, MD 21230
800–664–3848
www.lutheranservices.org

# SENIORS

*We do little good for people we reach out to unless we care for what they love as well.*

—*Maggie Steincrohn Davis*

Longevity increases every year. And those who are experiencing the benefits of a long life are asking lots of questions: When should I retire? What should I do with my optional time? How should I maintain productivity? The answer for many seniors is: retire when ready, then begin an adventure

- ● **Groups**
- ♥ **Families**
- ★ **Youth**
- ♥ **Professional Qualifications**
- ♀ **Training Required**

of service and charitable work for others. This attitude has led to a growing number of volunteer programs of which seniors are the backbone.

Other seniors, however, do not escape from the ravages of time. Instead, they find themselves as the focus of service.

This section will help seniors and those who want to serve them find a volunteer niche suited to their lifestyle and talents. The following are a few ways that everyone can make a difference in the area:

*Be positive about old age; cherish the future as well as the past and present.*

*Recognize experience, skills, and acquired wisdom in seniors.*

*Honor the role of caregiving.*

## Staying Fit and Involved

Effects of longevity impact everyone. You can serve others only if you preserve yourself. Here's a checklist for seniors:

• Avoid sitting for long periods of time.

• Maintain an exercise program: regular aerobic and flexibility exercise, plus walking as much as possible.

• Eat less: 1,200 to 1,600 calories a day for people over seventy.

• Drink eight glasses of water daily.

• Simplify your life; select priorities and set limits.

• Continue to learn; take a class or teach one. Read.

• Plan leisure activities and do them. (TV doesn't count.)

• Pay attention to your spirit; meditate on the meaning of life.

• Do things with friends and family; initiate rather than waiting to be invited.

• Be flexible; learn to deal with change, create new challenges.

• Stay positive; cherish the past and the future; write a life history; continue to make plans.

## Senior Volunteers

Retirees have experience from which to apply their cumulated skills in a more flexible, less pressured working environment. Retirement used to mean withdrawal from civic activity; but increased longevity in the last quarter century has resulted in twice as much volunteering by people over age sixty-five (see Robert D. Putnam, *Bowling Alone: The Collapse and Revival of American Community* [New York: Simon & Schuster, 2000], 129). Seniors today are utilizing their leisure time and better health.

> *Men who volunteer after age 65 live longer. . . . One of the greatest benefits is connection with others.*
>
> —*Douglas M. Lawson, Ph.D., author of* Volunteering: 101 Ways You Can Improve the World and Your Life.

Older people who currently volunteer are part of a cohort that have been active citizens throughout their lives. The generations coming up have a hard act to follow. Seniors are volunteering to act as:

- School tutors
- Hospital volunteers
- Foster grandparents
- Senior companions
- Community outreach specialists; education, mentoring
- Social service volunteers
- Entertainers in nursing homes
- Traveling grannies and grandpas
- Volunteers in retired and senior programs (RSVP)
- Hospice volunteers
- Missionaries
- Transportation providers
- Home health volunteers
- Elderhostel volunteers
- Rehabilitation volunteers

The government, faced with a new and growing challenge to care for the elderly, has created programs (such as the Administration on Aging and Senior Corps) to both help seniors and allow them to be helped. For a moderate stipend, people over fifty can volunteer for twenty hours a week (as well as receive transportation reimbursement) to be:

> It is one of the most beautiful compensations of this life that no man can sincerely try to help another without helping himself.
>
> —Ralph Waldo Emerson

- Foster grandparents who care for children with special needs in schools, hospitals, and other settings.
- Senior companions, who provide personal assistance to the frail elderly who want to stay in their homes.

Senior companions prepare light meals, read and write letters, or do whatever is needed.

## Helping Seniors

Many people enjoy good health until the last few months of life, but the person who ends up needing long-term care needs it for an average of 9.5 years. Help for seniors during the later, more disabling years of life requires assistance from many people.

> *Our society must make it right and possible for old people not to fear the young or be deserted by them, for the test of a civilization is the way that it cares for its helpless members.*
>
> *—Pearl S. Buck*

Families, neighbors, caregivers, and community services for the elderly all need the caring contribution of people who are willing to help. The list of needs starts simple and extends to full-time caregiving. The focus of all programs is to allow older people to stay in their residences as long as they desire. Consider one of these volunteer opportunities:

Make unrushed, friendly visits to senior citizens. Share stories with each other. ● ♥ ★

Help with yard clean up, lawn mowing, housecleaning, leaf raking, and snow shoveling. ● ♥ ★

Do home repairs. Paint an older person's dilapidated house. ● ★ ♥

Assist with shopping. ♥ ★

Deliver meals to homebound elderly. Sort, pack, and deliver food boxes. ● ♥ ★

Volunteer at Senior Centers—help with arts and crafts, dancing, computer seminars, aerobics, and so on. ● ♥ ★

Provide respite care to families coping with the stress of providing full-time care. ♥ ●

Transport older adults to medical appointments, to visit
family members in nursing homes, to obtain prescriptions, and so on.

Become a telephone friend to an isolated elderly person.

Help with Medicare, Medicaid, and Medigap insurance
paperwork.

Provide legal assistance (at a senior citizen law center,
for example). ♥

Make home modifications: install grab rails in bath-
rooms, handrails by outside steps, ramps, and so on

My patient was a large man, and the dead weight of his stroke made it impossible for
his tiny wife to move him at all. His son agreed to come over and learn how to do a
wheelchair transfer, but he came in looking so hostile I wanted to call off the whole
thing. He didn't even say hello. I explained that he had to grip his father in a bear
hug and then use a rocking motion to pivot him from the bed to the wheelchair. The
son went over to the bed where his father was sitting and put his arms around him,
just like I said. He got the rocking motion going, but then all of a sudden I realized
that both of them were crying. It was the most amazing thing. They stayed like that
for a long time, rocking and crying.

—Wendy Lustbader, from "Thoughts on the Meaning of Frailty," Generations

## Dementia and Alzheimer's

Losing your memory is not a necessary result of aging. Younger
people have memories like sponges but older people may have
minds that are more like filing cabinets. The older person has
also learned to filter the vast glut of news all around them; they
may not pay attention to what appears useless.

Many people with Alzheimer-type symptoms may have other
correctable problems. If you are helping someone dealing with
dementia or the early stages of Alzheimer's, keep these suggestions in mind:

Encourage elders with symptoms to see a doctor regularly. Much can be done for Alzheimer patients in the early stages through treatments and therapy.

Focus on the abilities the person still has.

Help the patient to keep a notebook with important information they are prone to forget.

Assist the patient to help themselves dress; lay out clothing and grooming supplies.

> *We can look for beauty and embrace our ultimate fragility any time we choose. Doing so would tell us what kind of life to lead. Once we begin living in terms of the question, "Who would take care of me if I got sick?" the whole of life transforms. The question mandates a shift in the order of things, making a life rich with generosity and kindness more desirable than any other kind of fortune.*
>
> —*Wendy Lustbader, from* "Thoughts on the Meaning of Frailty," *Generations*

The later stages of Alzheimer's can become a twenty-four-hour-a-day job for a caregiver. Volunteers can offer full-time caregivers assistance as they provide Alzheimer patients with:

- Physical care—feeding, bathing, helping the patient use the toilet and changing underwear
- A calm, predictable environment, which is essential to keeping the afflicted person's mood up ♥ ★
- Items to safety-proof a house; watchcare to prevent wandering ♥
- Companionship; visits from friends and loved ones ● ♥ ★
- Projects to keep them occupied—arts and crafts, visual stimulation ♥ ★
- Entertainment—audio and video tapes, someone to sing along with ♥ ★
- Affection—people who give love regardless of the negative impact of the disease ♥ ★

- Validation—acceptance of the way they perceive reality ♥

Volunteers can provide caregivers with their needs:

- Training in problem-solving skills and emotion regulation ♥ ⚹

- Visits from others; regular conversations with people in the outside world ♥

- Appreciation and encouragement from family and friends ♥

- A support network in which to vent their frustrations ♥

- Entertainment—something every day to laugh about ♥ ★

- Regular time off. ♥ ★

## HOSPICE CARE

Hospice is a program for the terminally ill that offers spiritual and emotional as well as physical comfort. Hospice workers are experts in staying ahead of the pain, one of the most common fears. A team of caring family members, friends, and volunteers can help someone through the dying process, allowing that individual the opportunity to stay in their home environment. Hospice service is also available through nursing homes and some prisons. Hospice volunteers may:

> When six years ago, I had my stroke,
> My room contained a crowd:
> Friends and family, grandkids too, all made me very proud.
> But time can change the best intent,
> It's very clear to see.
> I know they have their lives to live,
> But dammit, I'm still me.
>
> —By John Reiley, caregiver. "I'm Still Me" is written from his wife's perspective. She had a stroke 3 months after running the New York marathon at age 67.

- Monitor the patient's level of pain by asking questions: How much pain do you feel on a scale of 1 to 10? Where is it? What makes it better or worse? ⚹

- Listen to the patient. Strive to understand the individual's attitude and support it. Ask questions: What do you fear? What gives you hope? Or just sit quietly. ⚹

- Give the person some control; offer choices. What do you want to eat? to wear? Is there something specific I can do that would make it easier? ⚹

- Share stories and feelings as appropriate; use a clear, calm, low voice (half of people over 65 have hearing loss). ⚹

- Watch for nonverbal communication; look the person in the eye; offer touch comfort.

- Remind the individual that they are more than their illness. If the person asks "Am I dying?" respond by asking them, "What do you think?" ⚹

---

*Neither openness to experience, nor self-reflection, self-awareness, determination, or constancy need to decline with advancing age. They are aspects of an individual's personality rather than related to biological aging. But the longer one practices these qualities, the more successful one will be. . . . This is why growing old is a necessary but not a sufficient condition for the emergence of wisdom.*

—Monika Ardelt, Department of Sociology, University of Florida

---

## MORE IDEAS FOR EXPANDING SERVICE

Linking generations can strengthen both the old and the young. Facilitating constructive interaction is an important service. Here are some ides in which the two generations can serve together and, in turn, serve one another:

- Seniors can discuss their careers, hobbies or history with youth groups, school classes, younger neighbors, and grandchildren.

- Young people can write a seniors' biography. ★

- Young people and seniors can be pen pals or E-mail pals. ★

- Youth can teach seniors computer skills or vice versa. ★

- Students and elders can share a gardening project, plant trees together. ★

- Seniors can work with young people to make items for the classroom, the congregation, or the community center, such as easels, bookcases, puppets, and so on.

- Youth and elders may work together to write and perform living history theater presentations or build a community tree mural (see www.elderssharethearts.org).

- Children can create art projects for local nursing homes; schools may pair off with senior centers. ★

- Artists/art students can bring art mediums into Alzheimer's and dementia care centers, providing expression for those who have lost the ability to speak. ★

- Seniors can phone latch-key children before and after school.

## Suggested Reading

Barbara J. Bridges, *Therapeutic Caregiving: A Practical Guide for Caregivers of Persons with Alzheimer's and Other Dementia Causing Disease*, Mill Creek, Wash.: BJB Pub., 1995.

Beth McLeod Witrogen, *Caregiving: The Spiritual Journey of Love, Loss and Renewal*, New York: J. Wiley & Sons, 1999.

## Internet Resources

Administration on Aging
www.aoa.gov

Alzheimer's Association
www.alz.org

Arts and Healing Network (lists inter-generational community project ideas)
www.artheals.org/community/build/build.html

Elder Action
www.aoa.gov/aoa/eldractn-volunteer.html

Elder Hostel
www.elderhostel.org

Elderberry Institute (serves seniors and has senior volunteers assist to
    prevent premature institutionalization by remaining safely in their
    homes)
www.elderberry.org

Family Caregiver Alliance
www.caregiver.org

GriefNet.org (E-mail support groups supervised by a clinical grief psy-
    chologist/death educator)
www.rivendell.org

Hospice Net (for patients and families facing life-threatening illnesses)
www. hospicenet.org

Little Brothers—Friends of the Elderly (matches volunteers with elderly)
www.littlebrothers.org

Neighborcare (an all-volunteer, free-of-charge experiment in neighbors
    giving health-related service to their terminally ill neighbors in rural
    towns on the Blue Hill, Maine peninsula)
www.heartsongbooks.com/neighbor.html

## Organizations

Contact local county aging services, which assist in a wide
variety of programs, such as Meals on Wheels, Chore Services,
food box deliveries, Senior Centers, Foster Grandparents, Senior
Companions, and so on. To volunteer, you can also contact local
nursing homes, care centers, hospice providers, Volunteers of
America, and other local organizations serving seniors

Alzheimer's Disease Education and Referral Center
P. O. Box 8250
Silver Spring, MD 20907–8250
800–438–4380
www.alzheimers.org

American Association of Retired Persons
601 E Street, NW
Washington D.C. 20049
800–424–3410
www.aarp.org

Innovative Caregiving Resources (interactive videos for people with
    dementia)
P. O. 17809
Salt Lake City, UT 84117
800–249–5600
www.videorespite.com

National Institute on Aging Information Center
P. O. Box 8057
Gaithersburg, MD 20898–8057
800–222–2225
800–222–4225 (TTY)
www.nih.gov/nia

Temple's Center for Intergenerational Learning
1601 North Broad St., Room 206
Philadelphia, PA 19122
215–204–6970
www.temple.edu/CIL

# SPORTS AND PHYSICAL FITNESS

*In life, as in a football game, the principle to follow is: Hit the line hard.*
*—Theodore Roosevelt*

Exercise can benefit everyone. Physical fitness improves society. It not only assures a sense of individual well-being but it can also prevent chronic illness, disability, and premature death.

Sports should be as much

- ● Groups
- ♥ Families
- ★ Youth
- ♥ Professional Qualifications
- ☇ Training Required

about physical vitality, emotional well-being, and problem-solving skills as it is about who runs the farthest or scores the most points (see "Physical Activity & Sport in the Lives of Girls," The Center for Research on Girls and Women in Sport, University of Minnesota, 1997). And physical fitness is just as well accomplished through non-competitive activities such as aerobics, weight lifting, and brisk walking. Longer sessions of moderately intense activities or shorter more intense activities tend to equal out. Everyone can make a difference to the health and fitness of the nation by:

*Being flexible; learn to enjoy a variety of physical activities.*

*Remembering that everyone can improve their physical condition with positive support and personal effort.*

*Facilitating participation by others: time and place to exercise is not available to many.*

## START YOUNG

Children who grow up physically active have an initial advantage, thanks to parents and mentors. Adults can:

- Start exercising with children by age 2.

- Make games out of jumping, stretching, catching, lifting.

- Practice one-on-one learning how to play different sports.

- Keep play physical and fun: encourage neighborhood games such as Red Light /Green Light or Ghost in the Graveyard.

- Hike and ride bikes as a family.

- Eager parents do well to remember:

- Youngsters who *enjoy* sports will more likely stay active throughout life.

- Pressure to win at team sports might overshadow more enduring lessons of hard work and persistence.

- Respect for people—teammates, opponents, coaches, referees—is transferable to others: parents, siblings, teachers, and so on.

- Gracious acceptance of defeat *or* victory is a learned trait that may prevent a quitting attitude later on.

## TEAM SPORTS

Adults who sign up a child on a team are both rendering service and assuming responsibility, which can be taken personally or shared around. To help a Little League or other youth team, volunteer to:

- Provide transportation (promptly to and from practices and games).

- Supply needed equipment (as appropriate).

- Give support (attend games as much as possible).

Many community sports programs are made up 100 percent of volunteers. Such programs need a continuous influx of people to keep them running—the more volunteers the easier on everybody. The tasks are often not difficult or time consuming, but they require commitment. Volunteer positions may require you to:

- Organize team registration.

- Manage the uniforms, equipment.

- Promote safety (coordinate CPR and first-aid training). ȣ

- Coordinate photo day, trophies, camps, or tournaments.

- Coach. ȣ

- Referee. ȣ

## COACHES

The average youth sports coach spends eighty volunteer hours a season with his or her players (Fred Engh, president of the National Youth Sports Coaches Association). An estimated 2.5 million coaches in the United States head teams that involve kids between ages six and eighteen. The turnover is high for coaches—typically three to five years—and parallels the participation of a child (see, Kent Hannon, "Does Your Kid's Coach Know What He's Doing?" at *Sports Illustrated Kids*, www.sikids.com/sportsparents/coaching/coachknow.html). If you are interested in volunteering your time as a coach, recognize that a coach should:

> *Most people hope beyond hope that "exercise" will be fun and magical things will happen while having a good time. Folks—it just doesn't happen that way. The "fun" of exercise is getting into a smaller dress size, pulling the belt a notch or two tighter, and feeling great after a hike around the park or the golf course.*
>
> *—John Colman, in "Time: Its Importance in Your Fitness Program," The SuperSlow Exercise Guild, www.superslow.com*

- Be responsible for safety, learning, and training

- Model ethical conduct

- Teach young people health fitness and life skills: talk about the dangers of drugs (the National Coachathon Against Drugs asks coaches to spend time on it each week). Also point out (and model) that tobacco impairs lung capacity and alcohol encourages dehydration.

> *Knowing when to cheer and when to chill out can often be a fine line. Many wonderful parents successfully walk this behavioral tightrope, but many others blatantly cross the line. . . . In one Florida city officials are taking a novel approach to reverse this troubling trend. They're sending their parents to sportsmanship class. The catch? If the parents don't attend—the child doesn't get to play.*
>
> —Greg Bach, National Alliance for Youth Sports

In addition, a coach working with youth can do many of the following, making coaching one of the most enriching volunteer opportunities available:

- Bolster confidence and motivate youth.

- Encourage players to perform their best; recognize them for a job well done.

- Help youth set personal goals that are realistic and attainable.

- Teach concentration and relaxation.

- Teach young people to focus their attention, keep composed.

- Teach mental skills such as progressive muscle relaxation and breathing exercises, which they can use to relax under pressure in other facets of their lives.

- Provide perspective.

- Help athletes to separate their self-worth from their performance.

• Help team members to redirect their attention to the fun aspects of the game when they get stressed out.

• Prepare young people for success.

• Through mental rehearsal and visualization, show youth that positive self-talk and constructive thoughts can influence outcome.

• Teach young people how to put it all together and achieve their potential (suggestions adapted from "Activities You Can Do with Kids: Coaches Make Great Mentors," www.health.org/yourtime/features/coachesmentors.asp).

---

**Am I Doing a Good Job? A Coach's Checklist**

✔ I organize practices so that kids aren't just standing around.

✔ I have solid knowledge of the sport and the ability to teach kids new skills.

✔ I spend time talking to kids individually or in small groups.

✔ I pay attention to safety issues, including conditioning, equipment, and playing conditions.

✔ I never belittle a player, scream or otherwise use an inappropriate tone of voice. Instead, I criticize play in a sensitive, positive manner.

✔ I listen to the kids—and their parents.

✔ I give everyone a chance to play.

✔ I don't let winning become too important.

✔ I respect the officials, opponents, and the rules of the game—and teach players to do likewise.

✔ I try to make sports fun.

(Adapted from NASPE checklist, available at http://sikids.com/sportsparents/coaching/coachknow.html)

---

## COMMUNITY FITNESS

Sixty percent of adults have no physical activity plan, and more than half of the nation's teenagers get no vigorous activity on a regular basis. Over 60 million people in the United States are overweight—that's a third of the population (see "Physical Activity and Health," A Report of the Surgeon General, www.fitness.gov/execsum.htm). Most people want to get in shape, but don't recognize their options and don't believe they have the support needed to stay healthy. Encouragement within a community can spark individuals and families to start a physical fitness routine and contribute to the health of the nation. Volunteers can:

- Serve at health and fitness fairs and festivals.

- Speak in schools, malls, clubs, and churches about the importance of being physically fit.

- Participate or organize Fun Runs, Fitness Walks, and Volkmarches (*Volk* means "folk," and refers to the European tradition of family oriented, non-competitive "people walks," which are catching on in America. Walks are typically 10 K or 6.2 miles.) ● ♥ ★

- Organize celebrations that have a fitness component, such as a bike hike, run/walk, scooter or roller blade event.

- Sponsor sports days that include tournaments in golf, basketball, volleyball, soccer, softball. ●

- Provide fitness testing (strength measuring, blood testing, and so on). ♥ ⚣

- Lead aerobic workouts at community centers and churches.

## CHARITIES

Charities have capitalized on fitness participation. A plethora of nonprofit organizations host runs, walks, and races to support their important causes. Volunteers can:

- Participate (most races require participants to find a sponsor or pay a nominal fee that goes to support the cause of the race).

- Sponsor a participant. ♥

- Greet, register participants.

- Service water stations; cheer. ★

- Transport participants back to initial staging areas.

Check out one of the following Web sites for information:

1. Alzheimer's Memory Walk (www.alz.org/memorywalk)

2. American Heart Walk (www.heartsource.org)

3. America's Walk for Diabetes (www.diabetes.org)

4. National Down Syndrome Buddy Walk (www.buddywalk.org)

5. Race for the Cure (www.race-for-the-cure.org)

*Regular physical activity:*

*Improves immunity to minor illnesses*

*Reduces cholesterol levels*

*Improves quality of sleep*

*Increases mental acuity*

*Builds and maintains healthy bones, muscles, and joints (helps control joint swelling and pain from arthritis)*

*Fosters improved mood; reduces depression and anxiety*

*Helps control weight and improves posture*

*Reduces risk of diabetes, colon cancer, heart disease, high blood pressure (can reduce high blood pressure due to hypertension*

*May enhance effect of estrogen replacement and decrease bone loss*

*Protects many older adults from falls and fractured bones*

*Improves stamina and muscle strength in people with chronic disabilities.*

## MORE IDEAS FOR EXPANDING SERVICE

To perpetuate the enthusiasm that stems from a successful fitness event, individuals and groups can work within their communities to:

- Offer local aerobic and flexibility workouts; include childcare arrangements and transportation for older adults.

- Encourage malls, schools, and other protected areas to provide safe places for walking in any weather.

- Form watch groups to increase safe exercise in neigh-borhoods and parks.

- Acquaint people with accessible trails for bicycling, walking, and wheelchair activity (work to create them if they don't yet exist).

## Suggested Reading

Fred Engh, *Why Johnny Hates Sports: Putting the Fun Back in Sports for Boys and Girls*, Garden City Park, N.Y.: Square One Publishers, 2002.

Michael Yessis, *Sports and Fitness Success from 6 to 16*, Indianapolis, Ind.: Masters Press, 1996.

Porter Shimer, *Too Busy to Exercise*, Pownal, Vt.: Storey Communications, 1996.

## Internet Resources

American Association for Active Lifestyles and Fitness
www.aahperd.org/aaalf

American Association for Leisure and Recreation
www.aahperd.org/aalr

Games Kids Play
www.gameskidsplay.net

President's Council on Physical Fitness and Sports
www.fitness.gov

SI Kids (great articles on coaching kids, list of coaching standards)
www.sikids.com/sportsparents/coaching

Volunteer Solutions (volunteer event calendar that includes charitable walks and runs)
www.volunteersolutions.org/volunteer/calendar/

"Your Time—Their Future" (ideas for coaches and mentors of youth)
www.health.org/yourtime

## Organizations

Contact local Big Brothers, Big Sisters (www.bbbsa.org), Community Centers, YMCA (www.ymca.net), or the YWCA (www.ywca.org) to be a volunteer coach or referee.

Contact the local Red Cross for advice on conditioning young athletes.

American Sport Education Program (ASEP) (distributes training
    materials)
1607 N. Market St.
P. O. Box 5076
Champaign, IL 61825
800–747–5698
www.asep.com

National Alliance for Youth Sports (NAYS) & National Youth Sports
    Coaches Association (NYSCA) (2000 chapters in 50 states)
2050 Vista Pkwy.
West Palm Beach, FL 33411
www.nays.org
800–688–KIDS

National Association for Sport and Physical Education (NASPE)
1900 Association Dr.
Reston, VA 20191–1598
800–213–7193
www.aahperd.org/naspe/template.cfm

# TECHNOLOGY

*Any sufficiently advanced technology is indistinguishable from magic.*
*—Arthur Charles Clarke*

Technology is a moving target in an imperfect world, where computers are essential for progress but don't always work. Technical volunteers help schools and nonprofit organizations with their high-level technical skills, but others can help as well with their practical, organizational, research, and

| | |
|---|---|
| ● | Groups |
| ♥ | Families |
| ★ | Youth |
| ☙ | Professional Qualifications |
| ☇ | Training Required |

teaching skills. Everyone should keep in mind a few general principles before looking for volunteer opportunities of a technological nature:

*Think globally; consider the unlimited possibilities for giving and receiving service to increase understanding and solve problems worldwide.*

*Remember the unique strengths of both human minds and computers when teaching and learning computer skills.*

*Protect yourself and others from the glut of inaccurate information and smut available on the Internet. Source-less material has very limited value.*

*Work to equalize availability of technical training for all people.*

## HELPING A NONPROFIT ORGANIZATION

A recent study ("Wired, Willing and Ready: Nonprofit Human Service Organizations' Adoption of IT" by Princeton

*Steve Osemwenkhae is a high school student who recently applied for a graphics internship at a top-notch PR firm in Boston. "I didn't know anything about computers," he said about his first visit to the Computer Clubhouse. Now he says "They [the PR firm] seemed to really like my portfolio. I hope I get the job, but even if I don't it gives me something to shoot for."*

*—The Computer Museum, program profile*

Survey Research Associates) found that 79 percent of human service nonprofit organizations have E-mail, 77 percent have access to the Internet, and 49 percent have their own Web sites—arguably the best means of educating the public and gathering outside support. Yet technology doesn't stand still. For computer systems to perform well they need maintenance: old files cleaned out, new software installed, memory added, and databases updated.

"Techies" who offer their skills can infuse a charitable organization with higher efficiency. Volunteers are needed to:

- Do general needs assessments. ♥ ⚡
- Determine what kind of database is helpful for a particular charity. ♥ ⚡
- Design a database. ♥ ⚡
- Train staff to use a database. ♥ ⚡
- Update a database. ♥ ⚡
- Design a Local Area Network (LAN). ♥ ⚡
- Develop a Web site. ♥ ⚡
- Update a Web site. ♥ ⚡
- Document projects (record updates on databases and on new software installed). ♥ ⚡
- Check out usefulness of donated computer equipment. ♥ ⚡

Computer professionals who are volunteering in their spare time are wise to consider the following:

- Expectations of the organization (how much time will an assignment realistically take and by when will it need to be completed?)

• Upgrade proposals that include the least expensive alternatives, which is often all the organization on a limited budget can afford

• Use of language that is understandable to non-technical people

• A plan for gathering enough information about the present and future needs of the organization to know exactly what information must go on a database and/or what the Web site must communicate

---

*Don't let age determine a person's qualifications! The youngest volunteer I've worked with online was 14—he got through my arduous online application process and online orientation, "passing" with flying colors and went on to become one of my best online volunteers (he did lots of online research and offered feedback on various beta features).*

—Jayne Cravens, online volunteer specialist for the United Nations

---

## SCHOOLS AND COMMUNITY CENTERS

Many volunteer organizations have sprung up to offer children and youth access to computers in schools and community centers. Volunteers at these sites can:

• Offer technical career training in low-income neighborhoods before and after school. ♥ ⚦

• Offer forums for educators wanting to learn the best uses of technology in the classroom. ♥ ⚦

Schools typically have their own regulations that volunteers must follow, including a check-in procedure at the front desk, a name badge requirement, appropriate attire, and possibly a TB clearance. The school may also have special policies on security, confidentiality, and behavior (students' online access) which are important to learn up front. Once you've arranged to work in a school, you may be assigned to:

• Work with students on building computer skills.

- Train teachers, who may in turn make their own Web sites centered on issues and ideas that engage their students. 𝔯

Helping someone to use the computer takes patience. Phil Agre, an associate professor of information studies at UCLA, suggests that would-be teachers tell themselves the following things before they begin teaching anybody how to use a computer:

- Nobody is born knowing this stuff.

- You've forgotten what it's like to be a beginner.

- If it's not obvious to them, it's not obvious.

- A computer is a means to an end. The person you're helping probably cares mostly about the end. This is reasonable.

- Their knowledge of the computer is grounded in what they can do and see—"When I do this, it does that." They need to develop a deeper understanding, of course, but this can only happen slowly, and not through abstract theory but through the real, concrete situations they encounter in their work.

- By the time they ask you for help, they've probably tried several different things. As a result, their computer might be in a strange state. That's not their fault.

- The best way to learn is through apprenticeship—that is, by doing some real task together with someone who has skills you don't have.

- Your primary goal is not to solve their problem. Your primary goal is to help them become one notch more capable of solving their problem on their own. So it's okay if they take notes. (List adapted from "How to Help Someone Use a Computer," available online at http://dlis.gseis.ucla.edu/ people/pagre/)

## ONLINE VOLUNTEERING

Most online volunteers aren't techies; they simply know how to work efficiently online and have computer skills helpful to any number of organizations. Most applications for online volunteers are found online at the sponsor organization's Web site and will ask applicants to list their interests, skills, and language proficiencies. Options will be tailored to applicants' abilities; the decision to accept a specific assignment will carry with it a projected time line. Online volunteers may be asked to do a wide variety of tasks, including:

- Research on the Web, such as following economic trends, scientific developments, or news updates ★ ☒

- Servicing clients: making online visits, giving online advice on medical, legal, social, psychological or scientific issues, answering questions ♥

- Enhancing education: developing course materials and study assignments, giving instruction, helping with homework ● ★ ♥

- Sharing language skills: doing translations, creative writing, speech writing, text editing, article writing, and document summaries ☒

- Administrative assistance, such as developing proposals, doing accounting, light copy editing, and project planning ♥

- Using art skills to design graphics, perform desktop publishing tasks, or compose music ● ♥

- Offering professional and technical assistance: micro credit support, business planning, engineering advice ● ♥

*My husband and I had just moved to a small town in Texas, and I was somewhat restless. I graduated from Boston University with a BA in East Asian studies . . . I had always been very career oriented and was eager to begin. Before those plans got off the ground, however, my husband and I had our first son. . . .*

*I was able to do research on the Internet and learn about fair or alternative trade [for Netaid]. I am now directing and organizing the efforts of over 75 active volunteers around the world. Our volunteers range from high school students to Ph.Ds, "stay at home mothers" to record producers. They represent approximately 25 countries, on six continents.*

*—Laurie Moy, Coordinator of Volunteers for People with Disabilities, Uganda*

## More Ideas for Expanding Service

The types of service volunteers can give using new technology is unlimited. New ideas are being conceived constantly. Here are just a few:

- The Computer Clubhouse. These programs provide urban youth an after-school facility that is equipped as an artist's studio, TV newsroom, robot workshop, music studio, or inventor's garage. Youth have a place to be after school and also have the opportunity to learn new skills and showcase their talents. Volunteers help staff the clubhouse and offer assistance to youth in the program (see www.computer-clubhouse.org).

- Social service agencies in several states are offering on-site computer software classes for immigrants, dislocated workers, and people with disabilities. These classes teach literacy and other skills through highly interactive and engaging programs. Businesses may donate computers to the programs and mentors may donate time. (A distance learning program in New Jersey, "Learning How to Smile Online," by Nancy T. Fisher and Laura J. Frazer of the Jewish Vocational Service is just one example of such a project. You can contact Nancy or Laura for more information about starting a program in your area at ntfisher@jvsnj.org or lfrazer@jvsnj.org; 973–674–6330)

- Educational partnerships between K-12 schools and businesses, hospitals, and other organized groups are growing in popularity. In a partnership, businesses might meet with schools to offer technology internships to high school students. Hospitals might offer health care technology internships. Employees at dotcoms might volunteer to mentor students. The possibilities are endless.

> *Another online volunteering gig I love is mentoring a fourth grader (now a fifth grader) online at an elementary school in East Austin, Texas. Not having any female relatives that age anywhere geographically close to me, I was thrilled to get to know this student and share thoughts, hopes and dreams with her regularly. I hope she has learned something from me; I know that I have learned a tremendous amount from her. I had many misconceptions and stereotypes about young girls dashed because of my conversations with her. If most young people are like this student, the world is going to be an even more amazing place 15 years from now. And what's nice is that, even after moving away from Austin, I have gotten to continue this online mentoring relationship with her, something we both very much enjoy!*
>
> —Jayne Cravens, online volunteer specialist for the United Nations

## Internet Resources

CompuMentor (a resource on computer basics, databases, networks, hardware recycling)
www.compumentor.org

Computer Clubhouse (network of Computer Clubhouse locations for underserved youth)
www.computerclubhouse.org

Digital Divide Network (stories on advanced technology ideas to bridge the knowledge gap)
www.digitaldividenetwork.org/content/sections/index.cfm

Elderberry Institute (uses senior volunteers as "Com Coaches")
www.elderberry.org

Idealist.org: Actions without Borders (volunteering online)
www.idealist.org

The National Mentoring Partnership
www.mentoring.org

NetAid World Schoolhouse (U. N. site for recruiting online volunteers to help in developing countries)
http://app.netaid.org

TechSoup.org (the technology place for nonprofits; complete resource including volunteer opportunities and technology)
www.techsoup.org

Virtual Volunteering
www.virtualvolunteering.org

VolunteerMatch (U. S. site for recruiting online volunteers)
www.volunteermatch.org

## Organizations

MOUSE (Making Opportunities for Upgrading Schools and
    Education—an example is a New York City technology community
    that has linked students and schools to corporate and community
    resources utilizing many volunteers)
525 W. 120th St., Box 140
New York, NY 10027
212–678–8223
www.mouse.org

VITA (Volunteers In Technical Assistance— oldest program utilizing
    volunteer experts to answer questions of people in developing areas)
1600 Wilson Blvd., Suite 710
Arlington, VA 22209
703–276–1800
www.vita.org

# TRANSPORTATION

*For my part, I travel not to go anywhere, but to go. I travel for travel's sake.
The great affair is to move.*

—*Robert Louis Stevenson*

Transportation is sometimes essential and often therapeutic. The elderly, people with disabilities, and children may need special assistance moving very far from home. But public transportation doesn't go everywhere, and not everyone can afford it. Adults who volunteer to drive others where

- ● Groups
- ♥ Families
- ★ Youth
- ♥ Professional Qualifications
- ☒ Training Required

they cannot go on their own promote activity and independence. Everyone can make a difference to someone else by:

*Supporting neighborhood carpools*

*Driving defensively and courteously*

*Offering assistance to family members and neighbors who don't drive*

*Not driving when your age and mind have made it difficult to be safe*

## VOLUNTEER QUALIFICATIONS

Volunteer drivers log millions of miles every year. Some drive their own cars; others drive county or agency vehicles. Transportation volunteers are *always* in demand; and they typically like their work. Drivers make friends with people they transport by helping them in a very practical way.

> In my two years of volunteering as a medical transportation driver, I have found that I have the power to be a "smile maker." Volunteering for the Red Cross continues to be a rewarding experience in which the words "thank you" are more pay than anyone could give.
>
> —Bill Garrelts, Red Cross transportation driver

All drivers assume additional responsibilities when they transport others. Accept driving responsibilities for family members and close acquaintances only if you are protected with car insurance. Organizations that use transportation volunteers provide special training and requirements to ensure that the driver and passengers are as safe as possible. Driving an agency vehicle will simplify liability issues. Organizations that can't afford vehicles may carry a policy (in addition to personal car insurance) to protect volunteers. They may also reimburse volunteers for mileage. Most volunteer positions that involve driving passengers to and from any location will require:

- A current driver's license (in state)

- A reliable vehicle with insurance, registration, and inspection current (if using your own car)

- A clean driving record

- A personal background free from theft or violent behavior

- The completion of a defensive driving course (required by most agencies)

- A volunteer who is at least 18 years old; some programs require a driver to be age 21

Organizations will complete a driving check (and background check if required) and provide orientation and hands-on training. If a defensive driving course is required, it is free of charge,

> You really become attached to those people coming in for treatment. I pick them up at the airport and see the children's disabilities. I see the parent's reaction. Even when I don't speak the same language I see expressions of gratefulness in their eyes. And then I watch the improvement week after week.
>
> —Dean Manson, Shriners Hospital volunteer driver

often taken by video. The total pre-service training may take anywhere from four to eight hours.

## VOLUNTEER SERVICES

Driving an individual who is homebound or without transportation is a great service. This list of volunteer opportunities is evidence that your service will do another great good:

> *A lot of people don't understand the impact of transportation on the fragile population. One client told me, "If I hadn't found the Senior Transportation program I would have had to have a mastectomy. There is no way I could have found rides in to the hospital for chemotherapy treatments."*
>
> *—Pam Roberts, program manager, Senior Transportation Program*

- Volunteer with hospitals, medical centers, or the Red Cross for a block of time (usually four hours) to transport patients or blood and run medical errands. ⚥

- Take people with disabilities shopping, on errands, or to medical checkups.

- Transport cancer patients to and from a treatment.

- Take birth mothers to and from doctor appointments.

- Transport veterans and caregivers to and from VA medical facilities. ⚥

- Be a companion to someone who is visually impaired: take them shopping and describe the options, carry the groceries, socialize. ★

- Be a cancer patient mentor. Cancer treatment centers may match patients with a specific volunteer driver; appointments are made to accommodate both schedules. This mentoring service is invaluable for a child whose parents can't get off work for appointments. ⚥

- Be on call to provide emergency transportation to the hospital for young women who are pregnant.

- Join the Volunteer Transportation Network at a VA hospital and bring veterans who live long distances

from a hospital in for treatment. These are often
people with significant disabilities on a small, fixed
income who can't afford transportation. ✗

## SERVING THE ELDERLY

All states have some kind of senior transportation program for
people sixty and older, but that doesn't mean it covers rural, out-
lying areas or all urban needs. Sensitive neighbors can help by:

- Providing fragile seniors with rides to medical appointments.

- Helping the elderly and people with disabilities to go
  on necessary errands; running errands for them.

County services may also depend in large measure on volunteer drivers. (Some agencies offer services subject to the availability of volunteer workers.) Volunteers might:

- Escort seniors from their homes to the inside of their
  destination for medical appointments, dialysis,
  chemotherapy, physical therapy, and visits to loved
  ones in hospitals or nursing homes. ✗

- Drive seniors shopping.

- Shop for the elderly and bring the requested food to
  them. ● ♥ ★

- Deliver food boxes monthly to homebound elderly and
  people who are disabled—check how they are doing.
  ♥

- Deliver meals daily to homebound seniors. (Hot
  lunches need to be delivered Monday through Friday;
  volunteers deliver to several seniors one or more days
  a week.)

### Senior Drivers

Some of the most loyal, competent transportation volunteers
are retired citizens. As people age, however, changes may occur
in hearing, vision, flexibility, and reaction time.

There is a 55 Alive driver course taught all over the nation to help people aged fifty and up adjust their skills to compensate for changes associated with aging. The AARP is one of the sponsors and runs the program with trained volunteers. When the eight-hour course is completed, senior drivers may be eligible for a state-mandated multi-year discount on their auto insurance premiums. Most importantly, seniors who sharpen their driving skills can serve longer and better.

> *People with visual impairments have a terrible time. They may go to the store on a bus, but carrying their groceries back home is virtually impossible.*
>
> *Think of a lady trying to select clothing—she needs the colors described. These people are often suddenly homebound with no mobility skills. Without someone to help them they just give up.*
>
> *—Leslie Gerch, executive director of state Council for the Blind*

## Internet Resources

www.networkforgood.com (this site lists volunteer opportunities in your area)

www.volunteerconnections.org (Volunteer Center National Network)

www.volunteermatch.org (lists a variety of volunteer opportunities in your area)

## Organizations

Check with your county's Aging Services, Senior Transportation Services, Boys and Girls Clubs, Red Cross, hospitals, and service agencies for people with disabilities (especially services for the blind or visually impaired)

AARP 55 ALIVE
601 E. St. NW
Washington D.C. 20049
www.aarp.org/55alive/

Department of Veterans Affairs Voluntary Service Office
810 Vermont Ave., NW
Washington D. C. 20420
202–273–8952
www.va.gov/volunteer

# WOMEN

*Experience is not what happens to you, it is what you do with what happens to you.*

*—Aldous Huxley*

Unique challenges and opportunities face women in the twenty-first century. Women throughout the country tend to have lower-paying jobs and greater responsibilities for children. More women than ever before face the challenges

- ● **Groups**
- ♥ **Families**
- ★ **Youth**
- ♥ **Professional Qualifications**
- ⚡ **Training Required**

of abuse, family violence, and rape. Health struggles abound at all stages in life. At the same time, however, women are living longer, contributing more heavily to communities, businesses, and governments, and still succeeding at nurturing those around them. Everyone can make a difference to the mothers, single parents, career women, and battered women of the world by:

*Teaching young people that violence is not acceptable; examine and discuss how TV programs and movies glamorize violence.*

*Educating citizens to help make neighborhoods and communities as safe for women as men.*

*Supporting single women who are working and caring for children (assist with car pooling, watch out for schoolage children until the mother is home from work, and so on).*

*Being watchful of abuse. Notice injuries and encourage women in jeopardy to get help.*

## WOMEN TO LEAD WOMEN

Women who are homeless, on public assistance, or in prison and rehabilitation programs need someone to guide them in overcoming individual barriers. Strong programs embrace diversity and include women from a variety of cultural backgrounds. Volunteer positions include:

- Mentors ﹖

- Office assistants ﹖

- Public relations coordinators to write stories and develop media contacts for women's groups

- Support service contacts to provide phone counseling on available community resources or develop a library of reference materials for women to turn to for advice ﹖

- Workshop facilitators to plan and present interactive workshops on self-esteem, dressing for success, cultural diversity, conflict resolution, and sexual harassment ﹖

> *My role as Ingrid's mentor is one of support, friendship and unconditional love. Because her former life was built on distrust, building a strong foundation of trust between us has been a very important part. . . . Watching Ingrid grow and overcome her fears and obstacles without reverting to past bad habits has been a rewarding and enriching experience for me. Someday I know she will give back to the community by helping other women transcend their weaknesses and lifestyles that stand in the way of their health, love, and fulfillment.*
>
> *—Michele Patten, women's program mentor*

## UNIQUE SERVICE

Women are qualified for special service. For example:

- Nursing mothers can donate surplus milk to a milk bank (shipping the milk overnight in dry ice). For seriously ill babies, human milk is a medical necessity prescribed by a physician to treat immune problems and supply vital growth hormones. Donors must be in good health, non-smokers, and not be taking medications. A minimum of 150 ounces is requested from each donor (most donors start before their own babies are six months old). (Contact your local hospital for more information or visit www.health1.org/services/ milkbank.asp).

- Women who have had a mastectomy can volunteer to help others undergoing the same surgery through the American Cancer Society's Reach to Recovery Program. Women must be at least one year beyond their own treatment. Volunteers provide reassurance and practical help, including a kit containing information, a temporary breast form, and small exercise equipment. ⚲

- Anyone can give hair locks (men and children too). Locks of Love is a group that gathers hair for financially disadvantaged children who suffer from long-term medical hair loss (usually alopecia areata, which has no known cause or cure.) Several requirements exist for donation: ● ♥ ★

Hair must not be chemically damaged.

To cut, hair should be put in a ponytail or braid and then cut above the rubber band—it must measure at least 10 inches

The hair must be thoroughly dry before being sent in a manila envelope through the regular mail.

## PROVIDING ALTERNATIVES TO FAMILY VIOLENCE

The cycle of abuse hits women hard. Most of the mothers in homeless shelters come from broken homes with histories of alcohol and drug problems. Single parent families represent the fastest growing population living on the street. Without family support, many young women are thrust into society alone and tend to then enter into abusive relationships with alcoholic and drug-addicted men.

Other women may be abandoned, divorced, or abused and have children to care for. Several organizations and agencies have been created to help women in crisis become self-sufficient. A full range of services is needed, including day programs with referral information and emergency supplies, teen homes for pregnant and parenting teen girls and their babies, women's residential shelters, crisis shelters for battered women and children, transitional housing for single homelsss women and children. Organizations appreciate volunteers with a variety of skills and will train volunteers as needed to:

> **Facts on Domestic Violence**
>
> *It happens to people of all educational and income levels and all races.*
>
> *Male batterers are not violent in other relationships at work or with friends.*
>
> *A battering incident is rarely isolated. It usually recurs and escalates in severity.*
>
> *Attacks by husbands on wives result in more injuries that require medical treatment than rape, auto accidents, and muggings combined.*
>
> *Family violence is believed to be the most common and least reported crime. (FBI estimates 1 in 10 offenses are reported.)*
>
> *The average woman will leave an abuser 7 to 8 times before making the final break.*
>
> *70 percent of men who batter their wives also batter their children.*
>
> *79 percent of spouse abuse is committed by men who are divorced or separated from their wives.*
>
> *(Statistics Family Violence Prevention Services, Inc.)*

- Assist with individual and group counseling. ⚡
- Assist with educational workshops and parenting workshops. ⚡
- Provide comprehensive/age appropriate programs for children. ● ♥ ★
- Tutor teens.
- Assist clients with obtaining primary medical care and legal referrals. ⚡
- Translate and act as an advocate for women obtaining protective orders during court hearings and other client appointments. ⚡
- Provide clerical support for case and resource management. ⚡

- Give haircuts to women and children. ♥
- Provide pet therapy, art therapy, and recreation therapy. ♥
- Answer crisis hotlines and assist with crisis intervention. ⚩
- Make safety checks on women at risk by telephone. ⚩
- "Adopt" women and children for the holidays. ● ♥ ★

## PROVIDING HELP AND HOPE TO RAPE VICTIMS

While no measure is completely effective, a woman who educates herself about rape and sexual assault can substantially reduce the risk of becoming a victim; women may also train as advocates and educators at the same time. The need for volunteer service is always great. Volunteers may:

- Answer phones at a rape crisis line. ⚩
- Serve on a hospital response team for rape victims. ⚩
- Provide educational presentations to schools and the community. ⚩

> We have women arrive with their children and maybe only a sack of clothes, nothing for keeping house. We try to have sheets on the beds, dishes and pans in the cupboards, even a stuffed animal for each child [all donated, of course.] They walk in here where it's all safe and secure, see the way things are set up for them, and start to cry.
>
> —Security guard, battered women's shelter

Volunteers will learn how to be reflective listeners. Many will become confidants, trained to share a victim's shock and sorrow. The service may be emotionally demanding but the support to victims is essential. Some rape recovery programs depend on volunteers for 50 percent of their services. After training (about forty hours), volunteers may be asked to commit twenty hours of volunteer service a month in the speciality they choose.

### Internet Resources

American Bar Association Commission on Domestic Violence
http://www.abanet.org/domviol/home.html

Idealist.org (world service opportunities, including specialists in women issues)
www.idealist.org

## Organizations

Contact the local chapter of the American Cancer Society (www.cancer.org) for Reach to Recovery volunteer opportunities.

Contact local shelters, transitional women's housing, YWCA (www.ywca.org), or Catholic Community Services (www. catholiccharitiesusa.org) to help women in crisis.

Contact local rape crisis centers to volunteer.

HealthOne Alliance (Mother's Milk Bank)
Presbyterian/ St. Luke's Medical Center
1719 E. 19th Ave.
Denver, CO 80218
303–869–1888
www.health1.org/services/milkbank.asp

Locks of Love (hair donations)
2925 10th Ave., North, Suite 102
Lake Worth, FL 33461
888–896–1588
www.locksoflove.com

National Coalition Against Domestic Violence
1532 16th St., NW, P. O. Box 34103
Washington D.C. 20036
202–745–1211, Hotline: 800–799–SAFE
www.ncadv.org

Women In Community Service (WICS—programs to support women as they move from public assistance to careers with growth opportunities)
1900 Beauregard St., Suite 103
Alexandria, VA 22311
800–442–9427
www.wics.org

# YOUTH

*Each youth must forge for himself some central perspective and direction, some working unity, out of the effective remnant of his childhood and the hopes of his anticipated adulthood.*

—Erik Erikson

Youth represent America's future. That one in five young people lives in poverty and more than one in four lives in a single-parent home and is left unsupervised for substantial blocks of time on a regular basis should urge adults to action.

● Groups
♥ Families
★ Youth
♥ Professional Qualifications
⚥ Training Required

Providing safe, structured, and healthy activities for youth will make them far less likely to become involved in negative behavior. Given full opportunity, most youth will finish high school and go on to college, develop marketable skills, and volunteer for community service. The National Coalition for Youth reports that "youth who are involved in service just one hour or more a week were found to be half as likely to engage in a variety of negative behaviors such as alcohol and drug use, vandalism, and school truancy" (information available online at http://www.nydic.org/nydic/policypositions/service.htm).

The most positive youth programs are proactive; they encourage youth to participate in volunteering and are designed to support parents by enhancing their ability to raise responsible children. Everyone should be interested in the rearing and teaching of responsible young people. To make a difference:

**Assist youth through community and church programs.**

*Provide safe places for structured youth activities.*

*Mentor youth lacking traditional support.*

*Invite youth to shadow you at work; give them opportunity to develop marketable skills.*

*Include youth in service projects.*

## YOUTH VOLUNTEER OPPORTUNITIES

Young people respond to opportunity—not just to receive but to give. The number of youth volunteers during the 1990s soared. The civic involvement of the millennial generation is one of the brightest hopes for America's future. Youth who volunteer tend to be twice as likely to do so as adults (see Robert Putnam, *Bowling Alone: The Collapse and Revival of American Community* [New York: Simon & Schuster, 2000],122).

Opportunities in which young people (ages eleven through eighteen) can give service expand with age, but occur much earlier than

> *If you can . . .*
> *skip a stone*
> *sip a milkshake*
> *throw a Frisbee*
> *listen to music*
> *read a book out loud*
> *watch a movie*
> *sit on a park bench and talk*
> *visit a zoo*
> *shoot hoops*
> *ride a bike*
> *hit a bucket of golf balls*
> *Then you can change a life by just being a friend.*
>
> —Mentor Michigan Program Partner

most people realize. Several programs have no minimum age requirement when youth are accompanied by a leader. Possibilities, according to age, may include:

- For any age—beautification and trail maintenance in parks, beach and roadside cleanup, some office work, childcare assistance, sorting donations, delivering food boxes, making cards or crafts for homebound seniors, serving food to homeless, delivering books to shut-ins

- For ages 13 and up—interaction with children at care facilities, helping with tours and exhibits at children's museums, assisting youth with disabilities in recreational centers, learning first-aid or CPR to help in the community, working in public gardens, serving food at after-school meal programs

- For ages 14 and up—assisting with special events at summer camps, interacting and helping with homeless children, becoming a junior volunteer at a hospital, providing office support/preparing and sorting bulk mailings ℞

- For ages 15 and up—helping with construction and warehouse supplies for Habitat for Humanity, doing office work in medical centers/interacting with patients, sponsoring low-income children for Christmas, assisting with annual events in many non-profit agencies

- For ages 16 and up—assisting with sporting activities in recreation centers, helping with activities at senior day centers/nursing homes, providing tutoring services in math and reading at elementary schools, volunteering at a hospital, doing phone and computer work for legal aid services, recording books on tapes for people with disabilities

---

*I think kids really want to have a reason to live. And I think that's why gangs are so successful. There's a passion there . . . we underestimate the power—especially with kids. Kids are fervent; kids are passionate. Kids are full of emotion and full of fire to make things happen. Kids who have the opportunity to experience something on that level are much more likely to get involved in it—good or bad.*

*—Bill Brittain, Director of Matchpoint, Relationships That Make a Difference*

---

Many organizations keep a list of needs that make excellent Eagle Scout, Girl Scout, and youth program service projects. Such projects may include:

- Building or repairing shelves for food pantries, trail signs and picnic tables for camps, games and play equipment for child facilities, garden benches for nursing homes, and so on ♥ ● ★

- Planning donation drives for a variety of special needs: food/special-diet items, books for low-income families/adult literacy and prison programs, baby items for family centers and hospitals, hygiene kits for shelters ● ♥ ★

- Doing yard projects, such as painting or refinishing outdoor furniture for people who are disabled or elderly and for care facilities ● ♥ ★

- Distributing educational materials on child abuse, disaster preparedness, community education, and health ● ♥ ★

- Planting trees in parks or along rivers; watering trees in the summer ● ♥ ★

## SERVING WITH YOUTH

Many hands can join to accomplish more in less time. Integrating people of different generations and experience through service enhances awareness, understanding, and unity. Over the last decade, several national days of service have been established where young people and adults are encouraged to come together beforehand, plan what they want to accomplish, and spend the day working together. These service days are spread throughout the year.

> As a society, we must join together to meet kids' essential needs. There are countless ways that each one of us can get involved, right in our communities. . . . where we live, where we work—where we know kids by name.
>
> —General Colin L. Powell, Founding Chairman, America's Promise

- Make a Difference Day, created by USA Weekend magazine and the Points of Light Foundation, is held the last week in October. Adults and youth can work together on a community project or mentor a child this day.

- Groundhog Job Shadow Day, created by America's Promise—The Alliance for Youth, allows young people to follow professionals to see how education in the schools relates to the workplace.

- Join Hands Day, sponsored by America's Fraternal Benefit Societies, the Points of Light Foundation and the national network of Volunteer Centers, is the third Saturday in June. It has been set aside as an intergenerational day of service to the community.

## Community Programs for Youth

Structured youth activities after school, in the evening, and during school vacations are essential to healthy development. Youth need more activities than a school curriculum offers. They also need structured opportunities to explore social issues such as prejudice, and to gain greater respect for diverse peers. Through the generous service of volunteers programs offered at multicultural and recreation centers, Boys and Girls clubs, Kiwanis clubs, and vacation camps are all made possible for youth from low-income and at-risk populations right alongside more affluent participants. Help needed includes:

> *I wanted to volunteer for my tomorrow. My dream is to become a pediatrician one day in Liberia, West Africa, where I'm from. There are a million children there who need a helping hand. . . . I hope to continue this volunteering program and invite my friends to come join with me.*
>
> *—Klade M. Wilson, youth volunteer, St.-Luke's-Roosevelt hospital*

- Volunteer coaches ★
- Computer lab monitors and tutors
- Youth leaders to assist at dances and games
- Artistic volunteers to assist with ceramics, film making, music, and visual art classes
- Field trip and camp assistants
- Day care and after-school childcare providers

## Mentoring

Healthy values are the foundation of a productive adult life. Youth may not have sufficient role models or direct guidance to grow into independent adults. They may need mentors who can befriend and inspire them beyond the troubled world they see.

There are many types of mentoring opportunities and programs. Some focus on career goals and the transition to independent living; others focus on being a friend. Adults are most successful when choosing a volunteer mentor experience that fits their personality and schedule. They can expect screening, matching, and training if they work through an organized program. Most programs also require feedback and a number of joint activities with others in the program. Patricia Occhluzzo Giggans and Barrie Levy, authors of *50 Ways to a Safer World: Everyday Actions You Can Take to Prevent Violence in Neighborhoods, Schools and Communities* (Seattle: Seal Press, 1997), provide these tips for adults who wish to mentor youth:

> *The old have very limited interactions with youth; the young do not understand their elders or the aging process.*
>
> *The common bond of volunteering in one's own community is used to bring people of various generations together in order to start building relationships with each other.*
>
> —David Tetzlaff and Gina Zanin, *vice president and service ambassador for the National Fraternal Congress of America, members of the steering committee for Join Hands Day*

### Helpful Dos and Don'ts

- Do listen first and then talk.

- Don't make promises you can't keep.

- Don't try to follow a preconceived agenda; instead, follow your young partner's lead—support social activities and events.

- Don't be too impatient to make a difference. Focus on building a relationship first.

- Do be willing to work harder than your partner at forging a bond.

- Don't be discouraged if your partner is more lax than you about connecting.

- Don't ask personal questions before you have a solid relationship.

- Do be sensitive to cultural and economic differences.

- Don't focus on establishing a relationship with the youth's family members.

- Do provide support and challenge. Don't tell your partner what to do—help him or her work out a problem.

- Do be dependable.

- Do be realistic. You may not turn someone's life around, but you can make a small, worthwhile difference.

## AT-RISK YOUTH

Some teenagers leave home because they believe it is their only option for survival. They may have been victims of abuse for years. Others are caught in addictions leading them to crime and a violent lifestyle. Communities may have homeless youth resource centers for youth ages fifteen to twenty-one where they can receive food, wash clothes, take a shower, and do job searches on the internet. Teens may be assigned to live-in centers for alternative schooling and substance abuse treatment. Other youth, on target toward self-sufficiency, may move to transitional housing. Volunteers can help in any of these programs and may be asked to do the following:

- Assist with sit-down meals at drop-in centers. ★ ♥ ●

- Tutor in alternative high school settings.

- Share resume preparation and interviewing skills.

- Teach computer skills and research skills, such as how to collect and enter data.

- Consult on vocational training projects. ♥

## MORE IDEAS FOR EXPANDING SERVICE

Local organizations and individuals throughout the country are generating innovative programs in their efforts to equalize opportunities for all youth. Take a look at some of these volunteer ideas:

- A clown artist from the Gesundheit! Institute (see www.patchadams.org) teaches girls from a group home to entertain for birthday parties (to earn a little spending money) and at hospitals (to brighten up patients' stays).

- The Baltimore VA Medical Center sponsors (with HOYAS—Helping Our Youth Achieve Success) year-long internships for troubled high school boys assisted by mentors.

- An experimental art gallery in Seattle, Washington, offers painting, tap dancing, and sculpting workshops to kids in juvenile detention programs. (Contact The Experimental Art Gallery, Seattle, WA, 206–441–1768.)

- A "Working Classroom" group, based in Albuquerque, New Mexico, offers at-risk students training in art, the-ater, and creative writing to create bilingual plays about social issues and write primers for children in Central America (call 505–242–9267 for more information).

- A nonprofit entertainment organization in New Mexico invites teens to create and produce puppet shows for children and rap'n'roll operas for teens about construc-tive ways to handle conflicts. (Contact Working for Alternatives to Violence through Entertainment—WAVE—at 105 Camino Teresa, Sante Fe, NM 87505–4703, 505–982–8882 or see www.bullyproof.org/future)

- A ballet company in Santa Ana, California, invites children from the poorest neighborhoods into year-round dance classes, field trips, and workshops and provides free academic tutoring. (Contact Saint Joseph Ballet, 220 East Fourth Street, Suite 207, Santa Ana, CA 92701–4644, 714–541–8314).

- People commit to help second- or third-grade at-risk children who want a college education through a year-round program of tutoring, mentoring, and social activities that lasts twelve to fifteen years. (Contact the "I Have a Dream" Foundation at www.ihad.org.)

## Internet Resources

Drug Abuse Resistance Education
www.dare.org

National Mentoring Partnership
www.mentoring.org

Network for Good
www.networkforgood.org

Volunteer Center National Network
www.volunteerconnections.org

## Organizations

To volunteer, check with local Big Brothers Big Sisters groups (www.bbbsa.org), Boys and Girls Clubs (www.bgca.org), multicultural centers, Volunteer Centers (www.volunteerconnections.org), Volunteers of America (www.voa.org), and youth resource and treatment programs.

America's Promise—The Alliance for Youth (information on Groundhog
    Job Shadow Day)
909 N. Washington St., Suite 400
Alexandria, VA 22314–1556
703–684–4500
www.americaspromise.org

Angel Tree Mentoring, Prison Fellowship Ministries (formerly match-
    point, this group offers faith-based mentoring for at-risk youth)
P. O. Box 1550
Merrifield, VA 22116–1550
877–478–0100
www.angeltreementoring.org

"I Have a Dream" Foundation, The (long-term tuition assistance
    program for at-risk children)
330 Seventh Ave., 20th Floor
New York, NY 10001
www.ihad.org

National Collaboration for Youth and National Development
    Information Center
1319 F St., NW, Suite 601
Washington D.C. 20004
877–NYDIC–4–U (693–4248)
www.nydic.org

National Conference for Community and Justice (camps and conflict
    resolution programs that embrace diversity and support equal oppor-
    tunity)
475 Park Ave. South, 19th Floor
New York, NY 10016–6901
800–352–6225
www.nccj.org

Points of Light Foundation (information on Make a Difference Day and
    Join Hands Day)
1400 I St., NW, Suite 800
Washington D.C. 20005
202–729–8000
www.pointsoflight.org

# INDEX